Clyde,
It's your season
No More Limits!
St—R

FROM THE BUS TO THE BENTLEY
No More Limits

D1603793

Stan Richards, Sr.

Ghostwriter Anthony D. Diallo
Contributing Writer Chereace Richards
Edited by Laura C. Jackson
Designed by Patricia A. Jackson
Photographs are from the personal collection of Stan Richards, Sr.

ISBN-13   978-0-9816888-8-6
ISBN-10   0-9816888-8-8

Y-NOT Publishing
12138 Central Avenue
Suite 197
Mitchellville, MD 20721
www.y-notpublishing.com

Printed in the United States of America

FROM THE BUS TO THE BENTLEY

No More Limits

STAN RICHARDS, SR.

I dedicate this book to my sons Stanley Garnell Richards, Jr. and Isaiah Matthew Richards, who will never know my struggle of growing up in the "hood" of Washington, D.C. Daddy loves you both from the bottom of my heart.

Acknowledgments

I would like to first thank my Lord and Savior Jesus Christ for His grace and mercy in my life. This book couldn't have been done without You.

Thank you to my wife, Chereace, for being my queen, best friend and soul mate. I am thankful for your love, your wisdom and for always being by my side. I couldn't have completed this book without your input and support. I love you with all of my heart and soul and thank God for you every day.

Thank you to my sons Stan, Jr. and Isaiah for your unconditional love. Thank you to my mom for always showing me unconditional love and support. Thank you to my brothers and sisters for being by my side every step of the way.

Thank you, Pastor John K. Jenkins, for being my hero and my spiritual mentor from afar. Thank you to my nephew, Sam Martin, Jr., for showing me the 5LINX opportunity. Thank you, Tishina Pettiford, Lisa Cloud, Barry Donalson, and C. Anthony Harris for not only being my friends, but also my family. Thank you to the 5LINX co-founders Craig Jerabeck, Jeb Tyler, and Jason Guck for creating this amazing opportunity.

Special thanks to Min. Tony and Min. Deborah Leaner and Y-Not Publishing for making this book a reality. Thank you, Tony Diallo, for bringing life to my story. Thank you to all of my family and friends. Even though I didn't mention you by name, know that you all play a special role in my life. I love you all.

Thank you to my 5LINX family for the support and love. We will forever be connected.

-- Stan

PART I

Stan Richards

Chapter 1

My story begins on November 3, 1961, in the nation's capital, "Chocolate City." Benjamin Banneker, the man who is credited with inventing the clock and designing Washington, D.C. [after the original architect, L' Enfant, abandoned the project], was born 230 years earlier on the same date. I'm proud that we share a birthday. Most people simply refer to the District of Columbia, the federal city that embodies the Capitol and the White House, as home to the famous 1600 Pennsylvania Avenue N.W. address. The rest of us, who are natives and reside in various parts of town, know a different Washington, a less formal one.

The Washington, D.C., where senators and congressmen meet on Capitol Hill and dine at downtown establishments like the Old Ebbitt Grill or the Occidental Restaurant [formerly known as the Occidental Grille] is far removed from my experiences. Instead of enjoying a relaxing evening with the family at the Warner Theatre or shopping at Woodward & Lothrop for clothes and necessities, my mother might on seldom occasions allow us, if finances were available, to shop at low-end multipurpose establishments like the F. W. Woolworth Company or Morton's Department Store.

Since at least the 1940s, financial opportunities and a chance to share the American dream have been limited for poor people of color. Local African-American families learned to build networks from church groups, schools and other community institutions. Domestic work was one of the few types of employment open to a huge majority of people in Washington, D.C., back then. Very few were able to obtain quality government jobs, let alone prestigious careers. Middle-class society wasn't completely closed, but it didn't overly embrace people outside the status quo.

Leon Dash, a Pulitzer Prize award-winning Washington Post journalist for the story of Rosa Lee [Cunningham], once accurately wrote that "poverty is a phenomenon that has devastated Americans of all races, in rural and urban communities, but it has disproportionately affected black Americans living in the nation's inner cities."

I, Stanley Garnell Richards, was born in Freedmen's Hospital (now known as Howard University Hospital) and lived at Gerard Street in Northwest Washington, D.C. We later moved and grew up around Florida Avenue or the "hood" as some people call it. I was the second child and the first boy born to my mother and father, Doris and Veola Richards, respectively. They had five children together: Michelle [Martin], me, Timothy [Richards], Cornell [Richards] and Victoria [Mayo], better known as Cookie. My oldest sister Renee [Ridley] and my youngest sister Crystal [Jackson] have different fathers. I was closest to my younger brother Tim because we started out sharing a love of basketball, but in later years we would get high together. Tim and I were only two years apart. We shared everything--clothes, toys and even the same bed [along with Cornell, my youngest brother]. We were, and still are, inseparable!

I remember being around the age of 5 years old and living

with both of my parents. We still lived, at the time, on R Street near North Capitol Street and First Street, N.W. At this point I worshipped my father and loved the ground that he walked upon. I would sit on our front porch waiting for him to come home from work. He didn't own a car so he would get off the bus at North Capitol and walk down R Street. I would see him about halfway down the street, jump off the porch and run toward him screaming, "Daddy's home. Daddy's home!"

Veola Richards was the greatest guy during the week, but on the weekends it was a different story. He would get drunk and beat my mother for no apparent reason. Sometimes, in the middle of the night, I would hear my mother's screams as my father would severely beat her. My love and admiration for him would then turn to fear and anger. The alcohol would change him from my hero into the family menace.

Although my mother had limited employable skills and little education, she was a beautiful woman with an hour-glass shape. She kept our home clean and put food on the table every evening. As a child, I always wondered why my father would beat her and treat her like an animal.

I remember hearing my mom (on the phone) telling her family members that she planned to leave him because she couldn't continue to take the mental and physical abuse. One beautiful sunny day (while dad was at work), mom got us all together and told us we were leaving daddy that very day. On one hand I felt so happy (because of the abuse), but on the other hand I was sad (because deep down I loved my father).

She packed up all of our things and moved us to her parents, my grandparents, who lived in a two-bedroom apartment located at 14th and S streets, N.W. My maternal grandparents, William and Susie Ware, already shared their home with two children (my uncle Hollis and Valerie Ware). Thus, when momma brought her six children and herself to live with our grandparents, a total of 11 people lived in a two-bedroom apartment. We only stayed with them for a very short period because of the lack of space and the fact that my grandparents were also alcoholics.

I remember my grandma being a very beautiful woman who looked like Marilyn Monroe. She was a great person during the day, but at night it was a whole different story. She would get drunk and curse out everyone in the house, including my granddad. She would always accuse him of getting involved with other women. My grandfather, William Henry Ware, was the nicest guy you ever wanted to meet. Quiet and mild mannered, he looked like Billy Dee Williams. Yet, he too was an alcoholic. Again, my mom didn't want to raise us in this type of home so she packed us up and we moved again.

"He told me later that it was guilt that would make him come home and jump on me like that," my momma, Doris Richards, recounted recently about her now-deceased husband. "Veola was a very handsome man, and women were after my husband constantly. He would sometimes become flirtatious and mess around with some of them, spend a lot of money on them and not come home for a few days after payday.

"My parents fought like that too. Veola carried on so bad sometimes that I made up my mind to take my children. That's what I did. I took them and left. He never thought that I was going anywhere. He would say, 'Who is going to look out for you with all those children?' I just decided that I didn't want my children growing up and seeing us living in that condition. Besides, I felt that if he really loved me, he wouldn't beat me like that."

The devastating effects of alcohol and/or foreign substances on my father and maternal grandparents should have been a warning for me to continuously lead a healthy life and never allow alcohol or drugs to enter my life, cloud my brain cells and destroy my subconscious. Sometimes the sins of the parents or forefathers fall on their children and grandchildren!

I was generally a shy child with few close friends. I was average in build, kind of tall and slender, light-skinned and always willing to please adults. I described myself then as the light-skinned kid with the big afro and sad face. My teachers and the other adults I encountered considered me handsome and mild mannered.

I spent the majority of my childhood battling poverty and hunger as we relocated from place to place around the city. Sometimes we had to move because my mother was on welfare and she couldn't afford the rent. Sometimes we moved because my father found out where we lived and came stalking us. Sometimes there were other reasons that a little boy like me wasn't privy to. Looking back now, my mom was an American "shero" to me. Women didn't leave their husbands in the 60's and 70's, especially if they had six kids.

"I got a domestic job as a maid at the Hilton [Hotel] and saved my money because I planned to move. Veola knew that I was working, but he didn't know where and how much money I saved. I remember my father telling me that he would help me move the boxes and things just once to my parents' place. I had to make up my mind for sure that I was leaving Veola because my father wasn't going to help me move the things one day and move them back in a couple of days or the following week," said my momma, now 69 years old and still the matriarch of our Richards family. Her birthday is January 15, 1942, the same month and day as Rev. Dr. Martin Luther King's.

"God not only blessed me, but he blessed me to be a blessing to others," momma says proudly. That's the mantra shared by the family.

"I've been living here since 1976 in Brookland Manor Apartments [on Saratoga Avenue]. When I first moved here, they [the apartments] were called Brentwood Village. I just always felt comfortable here even when there was violence occurring on the outside. It never came to my floor or door. This has always been home to me. It is hard to find places of convenience. I like being independent.

"A lot of people ask me why I continue to live here. I know I don't have to, but I feel safe here. God has always kept me safe. I can control my own air and heat and have my own washer and dryer," affirms momma, to my chagrin.

I have begged and pleaded with her to move. She can stay with me or I can buy her a nice condo somewhere. She refuses to leave Northeast Washington and that neighborhood. Momma is content smoking her cigarettes and watching such daily religious programs as the 700 Club hosted by Rev. M. G. "Pat" Robertson, the founder of Regent University and the Christian Broadcasting Network based in Virginia Beach, Virginia. Momma currently allows her niece and my cousin, Cecilia Ann Rhodes, and two almost identical twin cats, Sebastian and Harriet, to reside in her simple, but tastefully decorated four-bedroom apartment.

Back in 1968, during the riots in Washington, D.C., following the assassination of Dr. King, we lived in project apartments on Quarles Street, NE. I was about 7 years old. During this time my father would come over in the middle of the night stalking my mom. He even kicked down the front door of our two-bedroom apartment a few times. I used to think he was completely crazy. Now I realize that the demons inside that liquor bottle contributed to his insane mood swings and violent outbursts.

1968 was indeed an interesting year to reside in Washington, D.C., as well as other urban cities across the country, especially for African-Americans. In the aftermath of the rioting, I saw smoke and burned buildings all over the city. These and other moments shaped my life.

During these times, for instance, my mom would occasionally get us dressed on the weekends so we could catch a bus to go cross town to visit our grandparents. We used to catch the bus at the corner of Kenilworth Avenue and Quarles Street, NE. I always sat up front on the bus because I was so fascinated by how the bus operated. I just stared at the bus driver and wondered what it would be like to sit in his seat and drive a bus.

Back then, Metrobus was named DC Transit, and all the drivers were white. All along the route to grandma's house, I could see the charred buildings on 8th and H streets, NW. The National Guard stood on every corner. As a young kid, I felt very confused. Who killed Dr. King, and why would someone do something like that to a nice guy like him? Why were people rioting and burning down all the stores in their community?

Having to constantly move and search for sanctuary in this environment affected the entire Richards family psyche and definitely dwarfed my educational development. I hated school with a passion because my siblings and I changed schools so often. I had no stability. As soon as I would get settled and start making friends, we would enroll at another school in another ward or sector of the city. I didn't even like the smell of the various schools although most of them were kept quite clean by the janitorial staff.

God bless you if you grew up as child or adolescent and didn't experience hunger. I wouldn't wish that on my worst enemy. It is truly a horrific, humbling and humiliating experience that remains with you for the rest of your life. Even now as a successful entrepreneur, the memories persist and I recall the days when I would steal food daily in order to survive.

Times were tight for my mom, me and my sisters and brothers. When both my mother and father were in the home struggling with their brood, Daddy worked odd menial jobs while my mother toiled as a housewife. My siblings and I had a lot of love for each other, and momma kept us close during the hard times. However, our harsh financial conditions didn't improve any when momma left daddy. Momma eventually became a welfare recipient. We went from economically bad to financially worse!

The first week of each month, however, was like Christmas to the family. I knew we were going to eat well then. I would wake up very early on the first of every month feeling happy and excited. Eating well meant momma taking us kids to fast food restaurants, like McDonald's for hamburgers, french fries and the works.

This was definitely a contradiction with the other 23 or 24 days of the month for the Richards family. By the eighth day of each month, the family would have to scrounge around for food and toiletries. Through public assistance and food stamps, in addition to momma's check every month, the family would receive some bulk items of surplus goods from the government like canned spam and corned beef, pinto beans, rice, cheese and powdered eggs. Considering my family had seven members at the time, these items would never last long enough to cover the entire month.

Around the first of every month, momma would send us to the Safeway with the food stamps. I would hide in the back of the store because I didn't want my friends to see me with food stamps.

Thinking back, most people in the hood sold their food stamps for cash or drugs, but not us. As much as we were ashamed of those food stamps, we were thankful for them.

Even with public aid, the refrigerator would often have nothing whatsoever in it. Perhaps a box of baking soda and a stick of butter were the only contents inside the refrigerator. Sometimes we couldn't find even that much. I can recall having to share a pack of Now and Later fruit chews [candy] with my siblings for dinner. Sometimes we would open the refrigerator seven, eight or nine times hoping against hope that something might magically appear after the first few times. It never did.

11

Stan's mother & father in 1963

From left to right:
Stan's sister, Renee; his mom and brother,
Cornell; his brother, Timmy; Stan; his
sister, Michelle

Stan (front row, far left) & the boys from the
neighborhood in 1970

Chapter 2

I probably attended more schools between kindergarten and junior high than most people do in their entire lives. Changing schools so much didn't instill a love of learning in me. Perhaps just the opposite occurred. In fact, I achieved success despite the odds and formal training that one usually obtains in a classroom.

Houston Elementary, located in the northeast sector of the city, was the first school that I ever attended. I began first grade and completed the second grade there as well.

As soon as I got settled in at Houston, we moved to 1838 15th Street, NW, and I attended third grade at Garrison Elementary School. We again shared the home of my grandparents (Susie and William along with my Uncle Hollis and Aunt Valerie). After a few months, we moved to 618 Kennedy St., NW.

I repeated the third grade, not necessarily because the work was so hard, but because of my lack of attendance. I was enrolled at Rudolph Elementary School at the time. Although students typically attend their neighborhood school, our frequent moves sometimes forced me and my siblings to attend schools farther away, which required extended travel (walks).

Sometimes we didn't go to school at all. If momma didn't

have the resources to provide us with lunch or a complete outfit to wear, she kept us home. Truant officers visited us on a semi-regular basis because of our poor attendance record at school.

School policy required all students to pick up their report cards in person on the last day. I walked back home praying anxiously that I had passed to the 4th grade. As soon as I got home, I opened the report card and saw the official, dreadful notice at the bottom of the page—repeat the 3rd grade. Crushed, I felt like a loser!

Around 1971, we moved back to 1838 15th Street, NW, and I transferred back to Garrison Elementary School to repeat the third grade and complete the fourth. It was there that I remember simply staring out of a classroom window and thinking to God that there has to be a better way. I didn't know then, but He would hear my prayer and answer me.

Due to no fault of my own, I wasn't a very good student at the time. Family issues kept me distracted despite my teachers' dedication and effort. Instead of learning reading, writing and arithmetic, I concentrated on the hunger gnawing at my belly or my worries about my father locating our new residence. Schoolwork couldn't compete with the harsh realities of my life.

When I was 10 years old, for instance, I lived at 1838 15th Street with my family and grandparents again. My house was in the center of two totally different worlds. To the east of my house, 14th Street on down to 7th Street, was the hard-nosed ghetto, (nothing but dope, prostitution and gambling). To the west of my house was 16th street up to 25th Street, where the upper-class white folks lived (the Georgetown area).

On Saturday and Sunday mornings some of my hood friends and I would get up early and head over to the Safeway grocery store at 17th and Corcoran streets to carry groceries for the white folks. I would carry their groceries home for them and they would tip me a quarter or 50 cents. Their homes looked so beautiful, and they always seemed so happy. I thought that all white folks were born rich and black folks were born poor.

After making a few dollars, my friends and I would head over to the McDonald's across the street from the Safeway to eat lunch. After a few cheeseburgers, fries and Cokes, we would go back to the Safeway and hustle groceries until about 4 p.m. Then we would head back around the way to our hood.

After I stopped by the house to show my face to momma, I would head back out to our hangout block, 14th and Swann streets NW. This block was like Las Vegas. People gambled in the street between cars, played card games, or sold bootleg liquor out of their homes. Swann Street was the spot.

The police would raid the block to break up the crap games, which were big business on that block. I learned how to gamble at 10 years old. My mother warned me against gambling but I didn't listen. My favorites were shooting craps (dice) and playing tonk (cards). Man, I had it bad.

One day I was shooting craps on Swann Street in between the cars when I looked up and saw momma staring me in the eyes. All of a sudden, she grabbed me by my afro and dragged me down the street. My mother didn't play, bottom line. Later I found out that my younger brother Cornell had snitched on me.

Whenever I would lose all my money gambling, I would

head over to my favorite corner at 17th and R streets, NW. There I would post up and ask people for money when they stopped at the traffic light. A lot of my friends couldn't hustle like that because they didn't have light skin and curly hair. I could make some good money (a few dollars) on that corner because I had this cute smile and the white folks felt sorry for me.

I would struggle for many years with compulsive gambling. Later on in life I would find out that my father was a gambler. I guess this is why momma never wanted us to gamble. However, my mother never talked bad about my father or his shortcomings.

Nothing had changed drastically in regard to my academics by the time I entered the 5th grade except the fact that I now attended Harriet Tubman Elementary School. This was the time, however, that I developed a love for basketball. I didn't have many friends and acquaintances partially, because I was always the new kid in school and partially because of my shy temperament. Basketball enhanced my life and made me more receptive of school in general. I had natural talent for the game. I was tall, lanky and practiced dribbling and shooting as much as I could.

One of my proudest memories of that period was making the school's team. I could hardly believe it! Basketball was becoming more meaningful to me even as I continued to struggle with my academics.

Based upon my low test scores and marginal attendance, I should have been retained in every grade and not just the third. I got over, however, with my attitude, quiet demeanor and handsome profile. Teachers at that time rewarded the quiet, nondisruptive students by promoting them to the next class despite their anemic test scores. Back then they would give you a "D" or passing grade for just showing up and keeping your mouth shut.

Although I might have been promoted and in the same class with children my age, my retention and educational skills were miniscule compared to the other students. Of course, I remember playing with other children and listening to stories, but somehow I missed a few fundamentals. Maybe I was absent the day a teacher taught a critical lesson. Maybe I was present but too hungry from not eating a proper breakfast to concentrate on the lesson plan. Maybe I just fell through the cracks like a lot of other inner-city children seemed to do back then and still do today.

Why do so many inner-city children fail in school, drop out and eventually become unproductive adults? Is it the environment? Is it a lack of strong parenting? Is it the educational system? I'm not 100 percent sure but I lean toward the educational system and parenting.

The school system trains people in the United States, not just in Washington, D.C., how to be dependent. We aren't cultivating a bunch of entrepreneurs or inventors anymore. School systems equip students with mostly interesting and sometimes pertinent facts, but not necessarily with what they need to survive as adults in an ever-changing world.

When I was in school, there was no Internet or I-Phone or MP-3 player. The only way to complete a research project was to visit the library, master the catalog system and read different books. Kids have it easier now. Everything is literally at their fingertips. They don't have to leave their homes or even their bedrooms to obtain information, photos and videos about almost any subject they could imagine. I think in some ways this has hurt our kids because a lot of them take these resources for granted and have become lazy as a result.

What hasn't changed, or changed enough, are the school curricula. Children in this country must be ready for global expansion. With technology, Africa and Asia aren't as far away as they used to be. U.S. students in interactive classrooms can communicate face to face with students in Nigeria or Thailand. Are we preparing our students enough with foreign languages? I don't think so. Are our children becoming bilingual? Can our kids compete with other children around the globe who speak two, three and sometimes more languages?

That's an example of what I'm talking about in regard to the basic educational system in Washington, D.C., and around the country. Why aren't students learning how to balance a checkbook or manage credit cards before graduating from high school? Mandatory classes should be available in every public school in the country because practically everyone in America has at least one credit card and debit/bank card. Although I had several math classes and teachers, I don't recall having a class that taught me about interest rates.

How helpful would it be if students attended a class on how to file taxes? These are subjects and courses that could enhance every child's life. Yes, geometry and calculus are important, but if you're not a statistician, engineer or scientist, you won't use these subjects in your daily life. Sometimes I think the system purposely keeps students disinterested and fails the masses.

Although I faced many educational struggles, basketball

gave me direction and joy. My first year of playing organized basketball at Harriett Tubman was great. However we lost the championship to my old school, Garrison Elementary. After the season, my
school scheduled an awards ceremony in May. I would receive my
very first basketball trophy. I imagined bringing the trophy home
and showing it off to my mother and all my siblings. Boy, this was
going to be my best day at school ever!

Then reality set in and the shame and embarrassment returned. I had nothing to wear for an awards banquet. I didn't own
a suit nor did I have special church clothes or even an extraordinary outfit. My wardrobe consisted of mismatched items, discarded
shirts and pants, and knickknacks. I confided in my mother, and she
implored my Aunt Minnie (Ware) for assistance.

The afternoon before the ceremony, my aunt arrived and
saved the day! She rushed over to our house in a taxi, took me
downtown and bought me an appropriate outfit for the awards ceremony. I felt blessed. I also remain thankful and still remember my
aunt's kindness today.

My Aunt Minnie and Uncle Garrison Ware enjoyed the only
true marriage relationship that I ever saw as a child. They had been
married for over 50 years. Aunt Minnie passed away in July 2007,
and my Uncle Garrison, who's still going strong at 97 years old,
resides in northeast Washington, DC. God works in amazing ways.
They looked after me when I was a poor kid, and I returned the love
in their senior years.

During the summer of 1974, I begged my mom to transfer
me back to Garrison Elementary. I wanted to play my last year
(sixth grade) there. Back then, Garrison was known around the city

21

for its great basketball program and its coach, James Hinton. Coach Hinton was the brother of former Washington Senators baseball player Chuck Hinton.

In September 1974, momma transferred me to Garrison, and it was on and poppin'. Every year Coach Hinton would select the team captain, who would wear #44. That season he chose me to be the captain, and I wore #44 proudly. Our first game was against Harriet Tubman on December 6th. I'll never forget that game as long as I live. We arrived at Tubman, and I faced a sold-out crowd of students booing me and calling me traitor. We ended up beating them that day but went on to lose the championship to Myer Elementary School that year.

6th grade graduation from
Garrison Elementary School

Basketball remained a fixture in my life throughout junior high school. I attended Lincoln Junior High School and tried out for their junior varsity team. I was thrilled to receive word that I had made the team as a seventh grader. I was the only seventh grader to make the team that year. Basketball was so important to me that I literally began sleeping with the ball at night. I played day and night and on the weekends. I played for the Amateur Athletic Union Boy's Club Team and any other place I could. In my impoverished life, basketball provided an outlet and a sanctuary.

My coaches, Willie Borden and Mr. Tom Jones, made our team pray the Lord's prayer before every basketball game. Thinking back, I thank God for these two guys who poured His word into me at such a young age. Today, my 9-year-old son Stan Jr. has the same love for the sport as I did. He asked what did I do when I felt nervous before a game. I said, "Son, always pray to the Lord before every game."

I wonder if Mr. Borden and Mr. Jones ever thought that by having us pray before every game, they would pour God's word into generations to come? I might have been a poor kid in the "hood," but I didn't feel poor when I stood on the basketball court.

9th grade at Lincoln Jr. High

From the Bus to the Bentley

Chapter 3

I played basketball nearly seven days a week just to escape the pain in my life. My weekly routine hardly ever changed. I had mandatory basketball practice every day after school. When I left school, I would then play some more basketball for the AAU Boy's Club. I wouldn't get home until around 8 p.m.

Only my younger brothers Timothy and Cornell actually saw me play organized basketball at a game with referees and other parents. No one else in my family ever came to the games to see me or support me although I would mention my games far in advance. My mother and father never seemed to have the time to attend the games. I guess it kind of bothered me because I would see all of my other teammates' parents and families in attendance and wonder privately why my parents weren't there.

During this time, I had two best friends: Chris Flagler and Kenny Bunny. I thought they were rich because they lived in a house, their parents had cars, and when I visited them, which was as often as possible, they always seemed to have food on the table or in the refrigerator. Their homes were well furnished and remained clean and tidy. Chris and Kenny would get lunch money while I always had to eat the free school lunch.

In a lot of ways, I envied my friends and their lives. Chris and Kenny had nice clothes to wear while I would wear the same shabby outfit week after week. Although they never teased me, the differences in our lives bothered me.

The native home of legendary hall of famers Elgin Baylor, Dave Bing and Adrian Dantley, the nation's capital has always been a breeding ground for raw basketball talent. In fact, inner-city kids growing up in the hood of Washington, DC, in the 70's looked forward to playing in a particular basketball tournament every year: "ghetto tournament."

After a few years, the "ghetto tournament" ended, probably due to lack of funding. One of my goals during the next five years is to bring back this tournament for our inner-city youth and completely fund it. I played in a lot of "ghetto tournaments" against stiff competition. I competed against former Washington Redskin punt returner and Notre Dame star Joe Howard. I also competed against Tony Paige, who later became an NFL running back, and Anthony Jones, who played for Coach John Thompson at Georgetown University and later made the NBA with the Washington Wizards [then known as the Bullets]. I might not have had the same skills and abilities, but my dreams and ambitions were just as lofty.

At 14 years old, I tried out for the city-wide Amateur Athletic Union [AAU] team. More than 100 aspiring basketball hoop stars competed for a mere 12 spots. Competition was stiff, to say the least. Out of 143 Washington, D.C., kids, I made the cut. I was so-o-o excited. You couldn't tell me anything!

We beat all the teams in our northeast region and won the opportunity to play in a cross country tournament in Las Vegas. My position was shooting guard, or Guard No. 2. I'm a lefty and I drained that long outside shot regularly. I could hardly breathe at the thought of playing in front of a huge crowd of people away from the District and traveling on an airplane for the first time in my life.

But once again I had a reality check.

Our AAU team couldn't afford to pay for the airplane transportation, food and lodgings. We hosted weekly car washes to raise money but it wasn't enough. Each basketball player's family had to come up with $150 to cover expenses. Where was I going to get $150?

I talked to momma once again and hoped that she could make it happen for me. She tried her best but to no avail. She had six other children to support as well as me, and taking $150 out of the family budget to send me to Nevada to play basketball was not in the cards. She then gave me one final suggestion: Call your father and ask him for help.

That thought had never crossed my mind. I never considered him a viable option. I had never really asked my dad for anything in life before. So I called him and asked for the money.

He simply said, "No problem!"

According to my father, he was proud of me, his oldest son, for making the team. The money would be in my hands soon. I told him that my deadline was fast approaching—about a week before the team was scheduled to leave for "Sin City." The week finally arrived but my dad didn't. After repeated unanswered calls to him, I got the message. He wasn't coming. I wasn't getting the money and I could say goodbye to ever playing basketball in Las Vegas. Needless to say, I was devastated. I hated my father for years after that incident, not just for letting me down but especially in the way he treated me.

Many males (and some females too) act out with strange or lewd behavior because of their fathers or the lack of real father figures. Adolescents have been known to turn to drugs, alcohol, gangs and even womanizing to act hard and perpetrate. Fathers have disappointed both sons and daughters repeatedly throughout history and they will continue to do so. Do you remember the classic Temptations song "Papa Was a Rolling Stone"?

Fathers and mothers should be in the home together rearing their children. I'm not saying that they should be unemployed and in the home all day. I'm saying that teamwork, just like on the basketball court, is most important in the household. Although many single mothers raise their children successfully, children usually do much better in a good two-parent household instead of a home where the mother must act as both mom and dad.

We see how movies and television portray men on the screen. They're tough, rugged, fearless and usually super macho. Think about such characters as James Bond, Shaft, the Mack, Jason Bourne and Michael Corleone. How do their actions suggest that men should act toward their women, fellow men and their children?

These characters are more like caricatures. Youth who grow up watching these images at home or in the movies get the wrong idea about men and fathers. Unfortunately, not enough fathers reside at home with their children to set them straight.

Somehow I managed to keep going forward despite my own father's disappointing behavior. As I entered high school in September 1978, basketball remained paramount in my life. I began to gain recognition as a star player at Lincoln Junior High School in Northwest Washington. My grades, however, remained abysmal. Although I still wasn't learning significantly or consistently in the classroom, I continued to advance to higher grades on the basis of my congenial attitude and good looks.

As I mentioned before, we didn't always have money for bus fare or school lunch. Therefore, sometimes I would get creative if I wanted to ride the Metro bus. I recall one day sneaking on the bus by going in the back door after someone had gotten off (in the hood we called this "hitting the back door"). No one noticed me or at least reported me to the bus driver sitting in the front.

After getting on the bus, I could usually find dudes in the back gambling, playing this card game called three-card marley. This was a game where one would take three cards (two black and one red) and flip them around. The other person would bet that he could find the red card. Most of the time I would observe while the bets were taking place.

One day around the first of the month, momma gave me $43 dollars to go downtown to purchase a pair of shoes called bass-wee-juns. This shoe was a popular penny-loafer style shoe. I had been asking momma for months to please buy me a pair. Finally she agreed. We were living at 1501 Park Road in Northwest Washington at the time.

I hit the back door of the bus at 14th and Park Road (south-bound) heading downtown. Once again there was a guy in the back of the bus playing three-card marley. First I just watched for a while. Then I started thinking, man, I should bet him that I can find the red card. If I win, I could double my money, purchase the shoes and have money for myself. I never thought about losing all my money.

After a few more rounds I decided to jump in. "I'll bet $20 on the card in the center," I shouted. I slowly placed my $20 bill on the center card and the guy said, "Turn the card over." I quickly turned the card over, and it was black. I was devastated to say the least.

The guy asked, "Would you like to bet again, young brother? I'll make it real easy for you this time." At this point I had a total of $23 left, and I couldn't get my shoes with just $23. I began to get real nervous about the whole ordeal. Should I bet again to try and get my money back? Or do I go back home with no shoes and $23? I decided to go for broke.

The guy started flipping the cards around again. While flipping the cards he chanted, "Red set you 'head and black set you back." Thinking back now, the reason he would chant was to distract the person who was making the bet.

I placed my last $20 on the card to the left and turned it over. It was black. Once again I had lost all my money gambling, but this time it was my mother's money.

I rode for a little while and eventually disembarked at 14th and Pennsylvania Avenue, NW, the middle of a busy tourist shopping intersection downtown near the Washington Monument, the White House and so on. How was I going to tell my mother I lost all her money gambling again? I started walking, and then I just stopped and looked at the people running errands, shopping or simply going from one destination to the other. They were all white folk, and they seemed to live good lives. A few couples walked about, but I saw many more families. I wished I could change my skin color and become a Caucasian. Caucasians appeared to be rich and happy. Instead of being indigent and black, I wanted to be affluent and white. Was I the only one who thought this way?

After a while, I hit the back door of the bus going northbound at 14th and F streets, NW, and headed back home. Upon my arrival, momma asked me, "Where are your new shoes?" I broke down crying and told momma that I lost the money (lying) out of my pocket. My mother put her arms around me and said, "Son, it's okay. God will bless us with more money." One thing I always loved about my mother is that she never worried about money. She has always been a woman of strong faith.

"My early childhood was rough. There were times when we didn't have food to eat and we had to go to bed hungry," recounts Cornell Craig Richards, better known to his friends and family as CC. He was born on Valentine's Day [February 14] in 1965. CC is four years younger than I am and just two years younger than Tim.

"An additional hardship was growing up in some crime-ridden communities as we moved around from place to place," CC says. "Some of the neighborhoods where we grew up were in the ghetto with some tough people. As a family we stuck together. We were real close, everyone, but especially us boys."

Although my brothers and I remained close, my connection to the guys I competed with in basketball around the city was coming to an end. They were starting to take the sport seriously and think in terms of getting scholarships to colleges and playing professionally one day. For me, reality kicked in again. I knew that my basketball skills weren't good enough for the NBA, and my grades would surely keep me out of college. I had to decide whether I should keep using all my spare time to practice and play basketball or get a job and make some money.

There's an old street saying: Money talks and bulls#*t walks! With that in mind, I decided to put down the leather ball and get a job and a uniform at McDonald's after school. During the week I went to school from 9 a.m. to 3 p.m. I would then begin my shift at McDonald's at 3:30 p.m. and work until 11:30 p.m. The schedule exhausted me, and that McDonald's job was by far the hardest one I ever had!

After a while, because of the long hours, I often missed school. I showed up just enough for the school to keep me enrolled and not list me as a dropout. At that time, the school system would allow you to carry over credits to the next grade. I was promoted again from Lincoln Junior High to Cardozo Senior High School on the basis of my demeanor and nondisruptive attitude.

I remember falling in love for the first time with my girl-friend, Theresa Southerland. I called her "Reese." She was the star majorette at Lincoln Junior High School while I was the star bas-ketball player. I went to her home in upper Northwest Washington after the games and met her parents. Her mother accepted me, but her father didn't like me at all. Reese also had a brother.

I thought Reese was rich like my buddies Chris and Kenny. She and her family lived in a house, had at least one family car and ate a hearty, balanced dinner each day.

The Richards didn't have any of these daily rituals, including regular dinner. In fact, I would have sworn that only the rich could afford to have dinner each and every night of the week. I wanted the middle to upper-class lifestyle so-o-o bad! I couldn't even properly verbalize it at the time.

Reese and I grew very close despite our socio-economic differences. We went steady throughout high school. I would sometimes daydream and envision a day that Reese and I would marry and have a nice home and cars as well as children to eat dinner with each night. I didn't realize it then, but what I really wanted was the type of family I saw on television, like the Cunninghams [portrayed by recently deceased Tom Bosley and Marion Ross] on Happy Days and then [much later] the Huxtables [portrayed by Bill Cosby and Phylicia Rashad] on The Cosby Show.

By the time we got to Cardozo, Reese had made the majorette squad, which was a pretty big accomplishment since the Cardozo Marching Band had a renowned, world-class reputation. D.C. residents treated all the members of the band like local celebrities. The band traveled out of town frequently. On one such trip, Reese apparently gave in to temptation and cheated on me with a horn player named Buster, a "pretty boy" with light skin. I was devastated by the news but still wanted to keep Reese as a girlfriend.

To her credit, Reese attests today the same way she claimed back then. Her story has never changed.

"Nothing happened with me and Buster," she says. "That was a rumor spreading around the school. Buster probably started the rumor, but he never got any! I'm sorry if that story crushed Stan's heart, but it just wasn't true.

"That was the only bad incident about the band," Reese added. "It was a wonderful experience to be a majorette for the Cardozo Marching Band. It was a lot of hard work, but it was worth

35

it because it was fun. I worked very hard to get in the band. I remember my parents having to get special permission for me to even go to Cardozo because my zone school was Wilson." She proudly maintains an ongoing connection to Cardozo and the band as an alumna.

Whatever happened between Reese and Buster, the incident served as reminder of my current status. At Lincoln, I was a major celebrity because of my basketball prowess. However, when I started Cardozo and exchanged my basketball sneakers for a McDonald's apron and paycheck, my celebrity status disappeared. As a star within the Cardozo Marching Band, Reese caught the attention of upperclassmen constantly. Part of me felt like she had cheated on me because I was a [McDonald's] nobody and I was losing her to the band and Buster. Still, Reese and I continued to communicate and date throughout school and long thereafter.

Mitch Credle, a lifelong friend, probably understands as much as anyone how I felt and what I lost when I gave up basketball. He remembers me from our Lincoln Junior High School days as being one of the best basketball players [at my age and level] that he had ever seen.

"We played for the Boys & Girls Club as kids," said Mitch. "Stan was one of the better players in Northwest. He was a standout! I think he made the varsity squad in the 7th grade around the age of 15. I had to wait until the 9th grade before making the team."

When I recount the tale of my first love and think about my high school years, I feel cheated. I lost a lot of my high school experience by working full time at McDonald's. However, I had no choice. My family needed the money. In addition, my often-hungry family welcomed the leftovers I brought home each night.

Some of my other siblings had similarly challenging tales about their educational struggles, particularly my younger brother Tim. "Because of the financial things going on at home, I went to stay with [my father] along with two of my older sisters, Renee and Michelle," Timothy Richards remembers. "Being away from the rest of the family was hard. It was away from my comfort zone. My father never beat us kids, just my mother. But... it was hard being there and living with him. He was an alcoholic and we were always on edge while living there."

Tim and my two sisters stayed with daddy for approximately six months. While there Tim attended Charles Young Elementary School in Northeast Washington before later following me to Tubman, Garrison, Lincoln and finally Cardozo.

Tim loved basketball as much as I did. I played one on one with him most of the time. We helped each other improve our games. Tim was a point guard who would distribute the ball and assist others in scoring. Most of my points as a scoring guard came from Tim's assists. I'm also proud to say that Tim was the only 7th grader to make our Lincoln Jr. High basketball team. The partnership worked. We've always looked out for each other.

"What's funny to me or may seem funny to others is the fact that Stan and I never had an argument growing up. Never! Not even one time as adults," Tim says proudly. "You would think that brothers are supposed to fight and argue. Not us."

What Tim and I did was support each other to become better as much as humanly possible. While I was on the quiet side, Tim was always outgoing and social. He was the true ladies' man.

"I always had a girlfriend or two. I have to admit to being a bit of a womanizer. I loved the girls and the girls loved me. I was always flirting or trying to get the females' attention," Tim laughingly recalls.

Our momma agrees: "Sometimes when Tim didn't go to school, girls would call here or come by upset. Tim was almost the spitting image of his father [and just as popular with the fairer sex]. When we went to Westmoreland, Virginia, to see Veola's hometown, the people stared at Timmy so much he got afraid. Their mouths popped open because he looked so much like his father. Westmoreland, Virginia, was the area that my parents originally came from, too. I was born in Washington, D.C."

Tim didn't learn any more in school than I did. His grades were as poor as mine. We just found different things to focus on. Basketball became my haven. Although Tim enjoyed sports and basketball as well, I think he enjoyed wooing the girls a little bit more.

"When Stan was in junior high at Lincoln, I was the [star basketball player] at Tubman. Then I followed him to Lincoln where I played more basketball. By the time I got to high school at Cardozo, I no longer had interest in playing ball. Women became my sport," Tim said.

By the time I became a senior at Cardozo High School during the 1980-81 school year, my absenteeism started catching up with me. I was absent from school frequently because after completing my eight-hour evening job, I'd sleep in bed the next morning. I was short on credits, and if I intended to graduate on time with my class, I had to attend both day and night school to make them up.

I faced a grueling schedule. I especially didn't like having to change my shift at the fast-food restaurant from the weekdays to the weekends, but I knew that my mother's biggest wish for me was to graduate on time with my class. I also knew that if I didn't graduate on time with my class, the chance of not finishing school was a real probability.

It still baffles me that some teenagers think dropping out of school and getting a General Equivalency Degree [G.E.D.] is easier than finishing the traditional way in the daytime with their class-mates. I'm not opposed to anyone obtaining a G.E.D. if that's the only way to get a high school degree, but it's definitely not easier than just buckling down and completing a degree one course at a time at a regular pace.

When a student attends night school or seeks a G.E.D., the pace is probably three times faster than normal. Just imagine the challenge of learning algebra, geometry or calculus at that pace. In addition, you only get one or two assessments during a G.E.D. or night school class as opposed to the numerous amounts of times and chances within a regular course or semester.

One particular teacher, Mr. Alfred Owens, stands out in my mind as not only my favorite but my most inspirational. Mr. Owens was my English teacher and the only educator who took me seri-ously when I went to my teachers that senior year and expressed my desire to make the honor roll. Maybe my expectations were unre-alistic based upon my academic record, but Mr. Owens appeared to have believed in me.

He told me the truth: I had a difficult task ahead of me, but I could accomplish my goal if I worked hard. I followed all of his classroom instructions, study suggestions and test-taking strategies. Mr. Owens gave me a lot of hope and encouragement that year. At every major point in my life, God placed someone there to encourage me to keep going. At this point in my senior year at Cardozo, it was my English teacher, Alfred Owens.

Unfortunately, I didn't make the honor roll my senior year at Cardozo liked I planned, but I did earn an "A" in English. I was so proud and elated. Most important, I graduated on time with the rest of my classmates. That was one of the biggest accomplishments in my life to that point. I learned an important life lesson from my senior-year experience: Ask for what you want openly and with conviction, and if God deems it right for you, you'll get it.

Chapter 4

Although I'm a native Washingtonian and a true lover of the "Chocolate City," the place had and still may hold some quirks. The nickname "Chocolate City" was coined after an overwhelming amount of African-Americans started residing in Washington, D.C., in the late 1950s and early 1960s. The city can be close-knit but a bit segregated on socio-economic lines. People in Northwest Washington, who arguably might have better educations and better-paying jobs, tend to only play and work in Northwest Washington, while residents in Southeast are even less likely to venture more than three to five miles away from their home base. Residents in Northeast might never share or appreciate the occurrences and trends in Southwest, and vice versa.

The irony is that a person might have more in common with a resident in another part of town than with his or her next-door neighbor. Sometimes that next-door neighbor shows less compassion to a nearby struggling resident than someone across town.

I remember an establishment next door to our home at 618 Kennedy Street, NW, called Al's Liquor Store. My mother knew Al, the proprietor. Al would extend credit to momma. She would send me or my older sister to get such non-essentials as potato chips, soda and cigarettes throughout the month. As soon as my mother would receive her welfare check, Al would cash it and take more than half the amount for the items purchased through credit. I could never prove it, but I always felt that Al, my mother's so-called friend, was taking advantage of us.

To be honest, I have to reiterate that I don't know for sure that Al cheated us in any way. It just seemed that after momma cashed her check, she had so little left over. We were getting only a few snacks from Al, nothing that should have warranted taking more than 50 percent of momma's check. The things we got from the liquor store were all perishable items that disappeared after one day. The cancer-causing cigarettes were probably the item that lasted the longest.

I also remember an Avon lady named Ms. May who would come to our house during the month with a car full of Avon products. I used to hate to see her coming. Momma used to say, "Go out there and help Ms. May bring her products in the house."

Ms. May was a little old white woman who drove a Cadillac full of Avon products. She was always smiling, and she'd give me a quarter every time I helped her bring the products in the house. Every month she had something new for momma to try. By the time she would leave, my mom had bought everything. On the first of the month, Ms. May came to collect a lot of momma's welfare check. My thinking was Ms. May was robbing my mother in an honest way.

Thinking back now, this is why I used to hate direct sales companies like Avon and Mary Kay. Now today, I love the industry that I used to hate so much as a child.

Of course, I wouldn't enter that industry for many years to

come. As I finished up high school, I had a more immediate problem: what to do next. I had already come to the conclusion that college wouldn't be my next destination. I was finished with my formal education.

I'm not saying that young people shouldn't pursue college. I urge all people who can succeed at college to go on and get that degree. Become a lawyer, doctor or engineer. I just wasn't one of those individuals. It took all my absolute strength to attend day and night school during my senior year in order to make up credits and graduate on time with my class. I knew that I wasn't academically or mentally ready for secondary education.

Viable alternatives to college were more readily available back when I was in high school than they are today. Besides attending a four-year or junior college, one could go to the military, join the Peace Corps or participate in vocational schools.

If you expressed interest in certain fields such as automotive mechanics or plumbing, you could start taking courses in high school geared toward that type of vocation and then after graduation pursue that study full time.

Although the District of Columbia is an urban environment, some students who had an interest in agriculture could work in the more rural areas of Maryland or Virginia. College wasn't the only option. Today, even with all the technology in existence, students seem to feel like they have fewer options. They can either be a nerdy geek or keep it real and go hustle.

A hustle used to be having a second job, perhaps on a temporary basis, because someone had gotten pregnant or recently lost a job. Nowadays, youth refer to hustling as dealing drugs or being involved in other nefarious activities.

After considering all my options, I thought long and hard about my future and decided on obtaining a good government job. Back then a good government position was the pinnacle, especially for the African-American, lower-to-middle-class residents in Washington, D.C.

I started applying for different full-time positions within the federal government while I was a 12th grader at Cardozo. I applied to the State Department and Labor Department. I even applied at the Federal Bureau of Investigations [F.B.I.]. Imagine my surprise and delight when someone called me in to take a test for an entry-level GS-3 clerical position at the FBI. This was during the spring of 1981 while I was still in high school.

Once again, I was so-o-o excited. I remember the test day like it was yesterday and not 30 years ago. I prayed on my way to take the test and I prayed all the way back home. Did I mention how excited I felt?

I was one of the few African-Americans at the J. Edgar Hoover Building taking the test that day. I was very nervous before the test and then again during the test. The exam was extremely hard. It was so hard, in fact, that I didn't even complete the test. The fact that I was a senior with very limited academic skills came back to haunt me. My mind sort of locked up, and I left the test site feeling like an utter loser!

While waiting to catch a bus to go back home that afternoon, I kept thinking to myself, "What am I going to do? What am I going to do?" I knew I'd failed that test. I also knew that my high school graduation would take place the following month and I had no realistic plan for my future.

I was still employed at McDonald's, and I had a part-time job at the U.S. Customs Service (a temp job for students in school) but I desperately wanted to leave the fast-food restaurant and get a stable job. Besides, I had been at Mickey D's [as the young people today call it] for almost three years. I knew I wanted something more in my future.

Nevertheless, I was still working at McDonald's in June 1981 after my high school graduation. I had worked on all shifts and mastered everything by now—the fries, hamburgers and cashier. I dreamed about Big Macs, Quarter Pounders and Happy Meals when I went to sleep at night. Although I was happy I had a job, I wasn't content.

Finally, to ease my suffering and anxiety a little bit, I got a full-time job as a mail clerk at the U.S. Customs Service. Slowly, very slowly, my luck started to change. My ship was coming in -- or at least I thought so.

In September 1981, nearly three months after my high school graduation, I received a letter from the F.B.I. I was shocked. This could only have been an act of God and nothing else because I knew I had failed that test!

I received an offer to work in the Bureau's clerical office. Man, I was so excited. God had really blessed me. I had no other explanation for this total good fortune.

On my very first day at the J. Edgar Hoover Building, I had to report for orientation like everyone else. It was both nerve-wracking and exciting at the same time. This was a stable job. No more smelling like french fries and grease when I came home from work. No more worrying about changing shifts. This was a regular 9-to-5 sandwiched in between a lunch break!

This was the kind of job my mother wanted for me. This was the kind of job I wanted for myself. This, I thought at the time, was my piece of the American dream. Watch out D.C.! Stan Richards is busting loose!

Before my probation period ended, I received an even higher position, a specialized training position called Fingerprint Examiner. Unlike the clerical position, I had a chance for promotion with this job. It started off as a GS-3 and went as high as a GS-7. This was definitely big time for me. I jumped right on it! After fully completing my specialized training, my salary increased to the GS-4 level.

I didn't feel like a loser at that point. I felt like the man! Once again, nobody could tell me anything. I was walking around like I was on Cloud 9 with my head held high in the sky! I felt good.

Go-go was always my favorite music. I grew up on it. This was a blend of funk, Latin percussion and rhythm and blues music created by District of Columbia artists and musicians from the streets similar to how hip-hop and rap are credited as coming out of New York ghettos. Go-go is something uniquely Washington, D.C., ghetto and not played largely on radio. You would have to attend barbecues in the backyard or go to dingy, crowded and small nightclubs [sweatboxes] like the now defunct Black Hole on Georgia Avenue to fully appreciate and enjoy go-go.

Chuck Brown is called the godfather of go-go music. The native Washingtonian is still as active and popular as ever today at age 74. He started playing five decades ago. If I had a theme song that identified my feelings at that particular point in my life, it would have been one of Chuck's.

I would probably have borrowed one of his classic songs, "It Don't Mean a Thing [If It Ain't Got That Swing]" which Brown remade from the illustrious Edward "Duke" Ellington, another Washingtonian. Some of the song's lyrics, which are dominated by a long, infectious band solo in the middle, are as follows: "It don't mean a thing, if it ain't got that go-go swing. You gonna do wop, do wop, do wop, do wop, do wah!"

Like that song, I felt joyous and jubilant. I told my momma that I was going to take care of her forever with my good government job. In my mind I had arrived, and there was no looking back. I bragged to all my siblings, friends and neighbors, saying I was hot and "U Can't Touch This," as Stanley "M.C. Hammer" Burrell would repeat a few years later in his 1990 classic rap.

I was making some decent money for the first time in my life, and I became materialistic. I got my first credit card with Woodward & Lothrop. I opened a jewelry account with Castleburg Jewelers. Everybody who was anybody owned a gold herringbone chain. I got one too along with a diamond ring and a Seiko LaSalle watch. After using my credit card for this, that and the other, I started to accumulate a lot of debt.

I probably went a little crazy! Practically every useless but expensive trinket that I saw, I wanted. I was spending more money than I had coming in. Forget about saving 10 percent of my income. I was a spendthrift. Sooner than later this would turn into a recipe for disaster.

Besides the change in my spending habits, my friends and associates began to broaden. I started to meet various people from around the country who began their careers at the bureau. Back then the F.B.I. didn't hire many local Washingtonians. Therefore, I became a bit of an anomaly—a young, friendly newcomer who could accurately give directions to city implants learning the Metro system or trying to find a landmark.

This small, unique reputation as a bureau resource started to come in handy with the opposite sex too. I remember the ratio being something like 10 females for every male employee at the F.B.I. That was pure heaven for me. I really started to lose my mind. Growing up in the ghettos of Washington, D.C., I never saw so many pretty and attractive black women in one setting before. Some were from here, whereas others hailed from the Midwest or the Pacific Coast. Some of the women were tall and voluptuous; some of them were skinny and petite. I was like a little kid stuck inside of a candy store with a huge smile

The ladies liked me especially because back then the light-skinned brothers were popular. I distinctly remember my ego rising and my head getting bigger than a fishtank thanks to all the attention I received.

1982 was a memorable year for me in many ways. I purchased my first car, a black Toyota Celica [two-door] Supra with key stone spoke rims and vogue white wall tires. It had a sporty look to it that I just loved. My DC license plates read "Stan-1." I drove in to work on Fridays just so I could show off my car. The young ladies liked riding in it too. Reflecting on that time now, I realize I was all front and no back. In other words, I was faking to everybody, especially myself, and seeking lots of attention.

That same year I also moved into an apartment. The apartment was located in Southeast Washington, D.C., on Call Place across town. It wasn't a particularly lavish neighborhood but it worked for me. Once again I felt like the man. I remember my mother and sisters giving me a housewarming party. During the cake cutting, momma broke down and cried because her first son was leaving the house and trying his wings. I hugged my mom and thanked her for all the love, support and direction that she had given me.

Life was pretty good for me at that time. I had a stable job. I had some first-in-a-lifetime possessions, including my automobile and a small, comfortable apartment to call my own.

Can you imagine a young man like me, a recent high school graduate with a good government job, a car and his own apartment? As far as I was concerned, those were all the essentials I needed. I was still a teenager and not legally able to buy beer in a nightclub or from a liquor store, but my future seemed bright and I was all smiles. Perhaps everything came too fast for me, and I couldn't go anywhere but down.

From the Bus to the Bentley

PART II

From the Bus to the Bentley

Chapter 5

My good streak started to come to an end after I had been on my job for six months.

I began having problems at the bureau. My problems centered on my constantly being late for work. As the oldest boy in the Richards' household, and in the absence of my father, I did any and everything I wanted. Nobody disciplined me. Momma had her hands full trying to raise my younger siblings with that measly welfare check she received each month. I probably could have benefited from having a stern male role model in the home.

Once I started working full-time shifts at McDonald's and making my own money, no one forced me to attend school or church regularly or anything else for that matter. In essence I had become a man in my household without earning the right. It was like being given the rank of general without ever setting foot on a battlefield.

Consequently, I wasn't a good timekeeper. I made my own rules. This worked for me in high school for the most part. I certainly didn't suffer any severe repercussions because of my tardiness and school attendance. I was still able to graduate on time. So what that I never received an attendance award! I only began to recognize that tardiness was a problem once I began working at the bureau. Before that I didn't really care. To be fair and honest, I didn't really care all that much at the F.B.I. either.

My head supervisor, Lamar Steele, was Caucasian like most of the other supervisors at the bureau during that time. The employees they supervised were mostly African-American or people of color. I remember my supervisor, whom I'll never forget, calling me into his office again and again. It reminded me of a troublesome pupil going to the principal's office each day for an infraction.

Mr. Steele would rant and rave and tell me that he would "bake a cake with me." That meant Steele intended to document every little thing I did. He was one of those types who dotted every "i" and crossed every "t." Unfortunately, I gave him far too much material to write down about my behavior and work ethics. I actually had very little, if any, work ethics to display. He could have written an expose' about my attitude and character -- or lack of it. As I said earlier, I knew that I didn't pass the examination and somehow felt, in the recesses of my soul, that I didn't really deserve this job, although I certainly enjoyed the perks that came with it.

Besides being late for work, I would take extended lunch breaks and sometimes would lose my bureau identification badge. The latter, I realize now, was a major infraction that could have jeopardized national security. Imagine if a terrorist today found an authentic F.B.I. identification badge left carelessly on a Metro bus or in a restaurant in the nation's capital. What do you think might happen?

I gave Steele cause for concern and alarm and enough rope to hang myself for miles. I gave him plenty of reasons to dislike me. In my mind, however, this white man was just picking on me because I was young and black. I perceived him as a sort of a bully and didn't take any responsibility whatsoever for my indiscretions. It's funny how a lot of inner-city kids grow up without any discipline, and when our poor character catches up to us we blame white people or try to play the race card. Sometimes I would leave work without completing my assigned tasks or duties. Sometimes those incomplete tasks and duties interfered with the jobs of others in the bureau. My reputation as the nice, handsome, young Washingtonian quickly changed into the immature man who constantly caused trouble for himself and others. By the end of my first year, the only people who liked me were the ones who hadn't come in contact with me and didn't know my terrible reputation. Everyone else viewed me as a menace or plague at the job.

Do you remember the movie Menace II Society, co-starring Larenz Tate and Jada Pinkett [who was not yet married to Will Smith]? Did you know that the late rapper and actor Tupac Shakur was supposed to star in that movie too but didn't after he started a fistfight with the directors, twin brothers Albert and Allen Hughes? I became, on a much lesser level, a menace to the F.B.I.

What was ironic about my job status was the fact that had the first director, John Edgar Hoover, been active and alive, no one in the bureau would have recruited me. Hoover left the bureau in 1972 and died nearly 10 years before I started my job. He retained the post of director for 48 years and had a reprehensible reputation of keeping long-standing, sometimes erroneous files on common citizens, famous celebrities and countless politicians and presidents, including John F. Kennedy. The late F.B.I. director reportedly trampled on the civil liberties of thousands of American citizens while in office.

Hoover, who was also born in Washington, D.C., like me, was a vigorous anti-communist who used the fear of communism and his office to compile information on people ranging from the genius Albert Einstein to Beatles singer John Lennon to Rev. Martin Luther King Jr.—perhaps his most despised subject. It was reported that the director hated Dr. King so much he refused to call him by his birth name or earned titles and referred to him as "that burr head." Hoover was said to have been devastated when Dr. King won the Nobel Peace Prize.

As a people, if we just continue to solely blame overt racists like the Ku Klux Klan or covert racist men like J. Edgar Hoover for our hardships, we'll never fully excel. In order to achieve full adulthood and become a real man or woman, we also must take responsibility for our actions or inactions and then, most importantly, go about doing something to rectify our misdeeds.

I was 19 years old, working at the Federal Bureau of Investigations and living alone in my own apartment [with daily visits from my brother Timmy and other close friends and family]. What I actually did was bide my time until the weekend where I partied and really lived--at least that's what I told myself back then.

I thought I was invincible. The party would start Wednesday evening and continue straight until late Sunday night. I started drinking heavily and smoking more than just occasional weed. Like most 19-year-olds, I just thought it was cool getting high and drunk as much as possible.

As usual, my brother, Timmy, along with an uncle and two cousins, Tyrone and Junior [whom we simply called J.R.], would hang out at my place. My uncle Hollis would just drink and socialize, but we younger guys [and maybe perhaps another friend] would mess around and use drugs. Eventually marijuana no longer satisfied us and we began experimenting with harder drugs, particularly snorting cocaine.

Remember I said that discipline wasn't my strong suit. I lacked willpower and restraint. I wanted to do everything immediately without waiting or gradually building up to it. I wanted to go to every party, date every girl and experience everything at one time. Imagine this scenario—a fat kid eating anything from a candy store and stuffing his mouth with treats. That chubby kid might feel great initially, but sooner rather than later that slovenly joy will turn into deep sorrow and regret.

Too much of anything isn't good for anybody. We can overindulge in caffeine, food and sex to name just a few potential addictions. Vices such as alcohol and substance abuse demand moderation or total abstinence. However, at that moment, moderation and abstinence weren't words in my vocabulary, and I didn't want to infuse them into my lifestyle. Moderation and abstinence were for the suckers and virgins, not for cool brothers like me who sported a blacked-out Toyota Supra.

I was familiar with nearly every nightclub or dank hall in the city. I would frequent a lot of the night spots that no longer exist, like the Chapter III in Southwest D.C. as well as Hogates, also in Southwest along the waterfront. Hogates, specifically known for its seafood cuisine and especially the crab cakes, has reopened and closed its doors on at least two different occasions since the 1980s.

The Black Tahiti and the RSVP were two more nightclubs

that I patronized from time to time. In addition, I would sometimes poke my head into the Penthouse on Georgia Avenue in Northwest Washington. The Penthouse [or simply the House as it is now called for legal reasons] is still one of the most popular strip clubs in the nation's capital.

I specifically remember being at Tiffany's one Wednesday night. This D.C. club advertised a happy hour during the middle of the week—"hump day." Tiffany's had special prices on drinks that night, and I was a regular. Wednesday night at Tiffany's was called "drink or drown" night.

Every Thursday morning I would wake up late for work with a hangover. In an effort perhaps to remain cool, I would smoke weed on my way to work. I would also smoke weed on my lunch breaks and immediately when I got off work. Stan, the cool, introverted teenager, had become Stan the marijuana man! It sounds corny but it was true. I was a pothead for real.

I smoked so much weed that by 1983 it began to affect me negatively. First of all, I began to slur my words while conversing with people. Initially I would try and play it off and kind of pretend that I was being cool and doing it on purpose, but people saw through that rather quickly. I also suffered with severe memory lost. I couldn't remember the simplest things. For instance, I would walk around the office or apartment for extended periods of time looking for my keys when they would be in my hand all the time. Sometimes I would look for my wallet or money and it would be in my pocket.

The most frustrating or scariest thing was my increasing paranoia. I thought everyone was out to get me and everything was turning against me. It felt like a conspiracy against Stan the man! I remember being very easily spooked at that time. I couldn't figure out why I had so many enemies and why they were all planning my demise. That's what years of intense marijuana smoking will cause.

One day I spoke to my Uncle Billy [Ware]. He saw the significant changes occurring with me and simply warned me off all drugs, but particularly cocaine, and reminded me that addiction was part of our family history.

"Stay away from that coke! If you like it, it will eventually make a slave out of you," he warned me.

But did I listen? No, I didn't. I didn't or couldn't pay Uncle Billy any attention. I thought I was unbeatable, and nothing like that would control my life. But I didn't realized that drugs had already become the most important thing in my life.

Cocaine was definitely king in Washington, D.C., by the early and mid-1980s. Later on something called "Luv Boat" or "The Boat" would replace the powdered cocaine. "The Boat" was a mixture of cocaine and PCP stuffed in a cigar or cigarette and smoked. It had a foul smell when lit.

"Luv Boat" soon lost its popularity to crack, which is cocaine boiled and created into a rock-hard substance and then smoked. The crack rock was highly addictive and caught on like wildfire. Those of us who had experimented with marijuana in the late 1970s couldn't really enjoy that high anymore. Perhaps we had become immune and needed a bigger fix. Perhaps since the stars and people I hung out with were trying cocaine, I wanted to keep up with the so-called "in crowd." Bottom line: I made the choice and can't blame anyone else for making me use illegal substances that would eventually destroy me.

My Uncle Billy was 100 percent correct when he said to stay away from all drugs and especially cocaine. It's very addictive. Ask the late rhythm and blues funk singer Rick James [who was born James Ambrose Johnson, Jr.] if you don't believe me. His successful music career, which included hit songs like "Super Freak," "Give It To Me, Baby" and "Fire And Desire" [a classic duet with the recently deceased Teena Marie; born Mary Christine Brockert], came crashing down after he started freebasing [smoking cocaine] on a regular basis. James once said that cocaine was the worst s#*t that ever happened in his life. It completely gripped his life and owned him.

The late comedian and actor Richard Pryor was also freebasing when he ended up severely burning half of his body in 1980. The popular entertainer did recover from the burn injuries but later died from a heart attack after being diagnosed with multiple sclerosis in the late 1980s. He, along with other deceased celebrities like John Belushi, Chris Farley and Kurt Cobain, all battled with drugs--particularly cocaine. They eventually lost their battles with drugs.

I loved cocaine. It was everything my uncle said and more. I was hooked right away. It gave me a false bravado. It gave me a sense of invincibility, like a conqueror. Cocaine lied to me and made me believe that I got confidence from it. It was pure evil! When I started using cocaine regularly, my arrogance went through the roof. Before that, in high school or thereafter, I had one steady girlfriend [Reese]. I wasn't a player like my brother, Tim. I never cheated on my girlfriend before cocaine came into and dominated my life. All bets were off with cocaine.

I started out only using the drug on the weekends when I did my heaviest partying. Within six months, I was using and snorting cocaine daily. I couldn't imagine life without it. I was in complete and utter denial. I would tell myself that I wasn't hooked and could stop anytime I felt like it. But I never remotely felt like quitting or even slowing down. The high was too strong. It kept calling and calling my name. Cocaine was my evil idol and master and I was its devoted slave and servant.

Back then you could find the best cocaine in Washington, D.C., about two miles from the Capitol on a street called Hanover Place. Hanover Place was the flea market and 7-Eleven for cocaine in the city. You could go there at any time to buy cocaine and find it open for business—24 hours a day, seven days a week. I remember long lines of consumers on both sides of the street.

As people walked down the street, the dope boys would yell, "a half or a whole." This meant did you want to purchase a half a gram of cocaine that cost $50 then or a full gram that cost $100. They had an orderly business operation on Hanover Place. For the most part, the dope boys and dealers kept people in line. Hanover Place attracted quite a diverse crowd, almost like a church or grocery store. You could find any and everybody waiting in line for a fix: blacks, whites, business executives, bums who hadn't changed clothes in days, heterosexuals and homosexuals. The one thing that the customers had in common is that they would come, buy their drugs and be on their way.

The cocaine at that spot was so good that I would buy a gram for $100, cut it with a food substance and then sell two grams each

for $100 and still keep a gram for myself. By cutting and resell-
ing the product, two things occurred: I was getting my first taste
of becoming an entrepreneur as an adult, and second, this probably
caused my addiction to grow twice as fast.

I loved getting high and having my head in the sky. Nothing
came before my addiction to cocaine. When I got that calling -- and
it seemed to come every waking hour of the day -- I answered it. It
didn't matter what day of the week it was or what I was supposed
to be doing, like work. When I got the call, I answered it immediately.

I started to go to Hanover Place on my lunch break to get my
coke. Instead of going to Florida Avenue Grill for some soul food
or the Shrimp Boat to get a crab cake sandwich or Ben's Chili Bowl
restaurant for a quick cheeseburger, I headed to Hanover Place to
satisfy my fix and snort a few lines.

One day I was so impatient and focused on getting "my
lunch" at Hanover Place that I forgot to take off the Federal Bureau
of Investigations work badge that I had pinned to my hip. Anybody
can tell you that it's not necessarily a good thing to let drug dealers
know your work place and full identity, but I was so twisted that
nothing else really mattered but getting that white powder and putting it up my nose.

During this time my brother, Tim, also partied at my side
and messed with drugs. He was both my friend and No. 1 sidekick.
Earlier in life we slept in the same bed together and then played ball
together. Now we got high together.

"No one forced me. I did it because I basically saw Stan
do it and wanted to be like him. We always shared things. We

both started smoking marijuana in high school, and when he got his apartment and started using coke, I did too," Tim plainly states.

"I didn't have plenty of motivation back then. I liked the girls, hanging with Stan and my other family members and friends, and that was about it. I didn't have any serious direction then. None of us did.

"When you're young, you think that you'll always be like that. Even though you might be able to see and read the warning signs in certain things, you're not thinking rationally. It's the choices you make that can affect you for a lifetime. The decisions you make now in your teens or twenties can change your entire life going forward," Tim says poignantly.

Tim had graduated from high school in 1982 and had begun working at a Quality Inn in Arlington, Virginia. He might not have been making as much money as I was, but he did have resources that allowed him to hang and party!

A lot of things were hazy to me during the height of my drug phase, which lasted from around 1982 to 1987. The cocaine really grabbed me in 1983 and didn't let go for approximately four or five years. Those years are like a tortuous blur. My singular fixation was getting more and more cocaine to feed my habit and keep me high.

I was so enthralled by the white powder that I started a part-time job to earn extra money to feed my very expensive habit. I became a nighttime van driver at the Quality Inn (where Tim worked) to make some additional money. If someone had sat me down and probed me for an answer, I would have had to admit that deep down I wanted some help. I knew that I was in the bowels of this cocaine habit that held me like a vise grip, but I was perplexed as to how I

From the Bus to the Bentley

could escape. I was absolutely ashamed of my dark secret.

Chapter 6

Besides ignorance, pride kept me from seeking professional help for my addiction. Every time I got paid at the Federal Bureau of Investigations, I would hear the incessant call coming from the cocaine: "Stan...Stan...Stan...Stan."

I shared my dark secret of addiction with my sister Michelle and she looked into rehabilitation for me. But what if the F.B.I. found out about my drug problem? The bureau would probably fire me immediately.

Ironically, if I had been thinking clearly, I would come forward on my own and asked for help from the bureau instead of dealing with this humongous problem privately. I might have qualified for some special type of program within the F.B.I. for stressed-out employees who had succumbed to substance abuse. I'm not sure if any such program existed, but I was reluctant to try. With my history on the job and the disdain that people had for me at the Hoover Building, I figured that I'd be an easy mark. Therefore, I never told anyone there at the F.B.I.

Sometimes I'd try and shake my daily drug habit on my own. Unfortunately, that was an exercise in pure futility. I began to be late with all of my other bills, including my rent and car note, in order to have extra money for my drug dealer. I probably had a $500-$1,000 a week habit. Cocaine became my mistress, and I spoiled her!

In 1986, I finally admitted to myself that drugs, and particularly cocaine, had a complete hold over me when the University of Maryland basketball star Len Bias died suddenly from an apparent cocaine overdose that largely contributed to a heart attack. He was just 22 years old, and the Boston Celtics had just recently drafted him to play professional basketball when the tragedy occurred.

I didn't want my mother to have to identify me in the hospital morgue as a victim of a drug overdose. But I couldn't stop! I took a break for a total of five to seven days. My inability to walk away from drugs scared me.

Something else occurred during my cocaine phase that was kind of significant: My father, Veola Richards, died from a massive heart attack on January 13, 1984. He was just 48 years old. His death was only somewhat significant because it didn't feel like a major tragedy to me. I took my portion of his retirement money and savings and spent it all quickly on my constant pursuit of cocaine. I was 23 years old at the time of his passing, and for all intents and purposes, we were two strangers.

I never really got to know my father, and we never got a chance to fix our relationship before his death. Tim and a couple of my sisters knew him better than I did. He would come around occasionally when I was still a boy, but most of the time he'd be drunk. Whenever he took me to the barbershop or to visit a family member or someone, I'd be sick to my stomach at the thought of being with him.

After he disappointed me with my Las Vegas basketball trip, our relationship really soured. I remember one incident that occurred on a Metro bus. I was sitting in the back of the bus coming from downtown on the way home. Halfway on my journey, my father boarded the bus and took a seat near the front. The bus was full enough that he didn't notice me in the back, but I never called out or acknowledged him. He got off the bus before I did without ever knowing that his oldest son was riding with him on the same bus that day.

For years I wondered why I had so much animosity toward him that I didn't want to even acknowledge him on a public bus. I've come to the conclusion it was because I didn't really know my father. I knew his name and could physically identify him on the street, but he was essentially a stranger to me.

My favorite holiday recollection, however, centers on my father and Christmas 1971. That was the year I got my first bicycle. That was so awesome. I was so happy. The bike was orange. I later found out that my father's friend, Charles Polly, actually bought the bike for me and my father merely took the credit.

Whatever the case, I hold no grudges toward Veola Richards and hope that he now rests in peace. At the very least, he doesn't have to continue his daily [and losing] battle with alcohol.

I wish I could have been able to call my father my No. 1 male role model as a youth, but I can't. One of the people I do remember as a role model and hero growing up was former Washington, D.C., Mayor Marion S. Barry, Jr. He's presently the Ward 8 council member in the city presiding over areas in Southeast Washington that are the most disenfranchised. Barry, who was sarcastically dubbed the "Mayor-for-Life" by the Washington City Paper, always stood up for what he believed was right, despite the odds, and never bowed to the Caucasians. Mayor Barry did a lot of good for Washington, D.C., back in the day, including helping the elderly as well as the youth get summer jobs.

The now 74-year-old Barry isn't a native Washingtonian. He was actually born in Itta Bena, Mississippi, before his mother moved the family to Memphis after splitting with his father, Barry Sr. The young Barry, on all accounts, was a gifted student who was very active in the advancement of civil rights for African-Americans. He attended and graduated from LeMoyne[-Owen] College in 1958. Later the student activist earned a master's of science in organic chemistry from Fisk University and became a chairman of the Student Nonviolent Coordinating Committee [SNCC].

In 1965, Barry moved to Washington, D.C., to open an office for SNCC. Soon thereafter he became entrenched with local politics and got voted onto the school board. During those years, he married and divorced his second and third wives [Mary M. Treadwell and Effi Slaughter, respectively]. Barry had met, married and divorced his first wife [Blantie Evans] while in school. Most recently, Barry married and divorced Cora Masters. He has just one son, Christopher Barry, whose mother was Effi Barry. She died in 2007 after losing an 18-month battle with acute myeloid leukemia.

After helping to quell further riots in the city stemming from Reverend King's assassination, Barry succeeded in his bid for an at-large council member position. He then later campaigned and became Washington's first elected mayor in 1979 and won two more consecutive mayoral terms before his infamous 1990 Vista [Hotel] Sting incident where he was videotaped smoking a crack pipe with the hopes of having sex with a former model and lover, Hazel Diane

"Rasheeda" Moore.

I stood by Barry then as I do so today. I, like thousands of Washingtonians, felt the mayor was a victim of conspiracy. Former U.S. Attorney Joseph diGenova spent fruitless years and several thousands of dollars attempting to jail Barry and, to diGenova's chagrin, couldn't get the mayor on even a parking ticket. DiGenova spouted accusation after accusation about Barry to no avail. People in this city remember that.

Even after succumbing to Moore's entrapment, facing the embarrassment of that disgraceful videotape and being jailed for six months, Barry was able to win a fourth term as mayor in 1995 when he won the city-wide elections despite the contempt of practically every white resident in the nation's capital and the backlash from the media. Marion Barry is the true man. He is invincible!

We [my siblings and I] always got summer jobs through Mayor Barry's program. I got my first job at the age of 14 and continued to get jobs until I finished high school. My family and I were grateful for those jobs. Not only did we learn some basic filing and office management, but the work kept us focused and out of trouble—or out of at least some trouble.

"Stan was always ambitious. He got his first job as a summer student at the D.C. General Hospital. Stan was working as a janitor. He helped me out by saving his money and using it to buy some of his school clothes," momma said.

My heroes and role models today consist of two people: President Barack Obama and my pastor, John Jenkins. Both men have overcome adversity, jealousy and insurmountable odds to become leaders of men and inspirations to young and old, male or female.

Barack Hussein Obama II was born about three months before me on August 4, 1961. He is the 44th president of the United States and the 2009 Nobel Peace Prize laureate. The president is also a lefty like me. Born in Honolulu, Obama is a graduate of Columbia University and Harvard Law School. Before becoming president, Obama was a senator and a Congressman representing the state of Illinois, where he resided for several years.

Besides being the first African-American president [his mother was a white American from Kansas and his father was a black African from Kenya], Obama is the first president to hail from the 50th state of Hawaii. Obama is also the first president to have to deal with so many international and domestic crises within two years of his inauguration.

The president appears to be a fine role model for me and everyone else. He is happily married to beautiful First Lady Michelle Robinson Obama and has two daughters, Malia and Sasha. One of the things I like most about him is the fact that he is a sports fan who thoroughly enjoys basketball--both watching and participating.

John K. Jenkins, Sr. serves as senior pastor of First Baptist Church of Glenarden [in Maryland] with campuses in Landover and Upper Marlboro. I attend services in Upper Marlboro. Jenkins has been the senior pastor since 1989. He and his wife Trina are the proud parents of six children and one granddaughter. Jenkins was installed as the church's seventh senior pastor [shepherd] after the death of Jenkins' mentor, Dr. John W. Johnson.

I started attending his church in 1994 with my first wife. Since that time, pastor has always challenged me from the pulpit to do the right thing and stay on the right path. He also inspired and encouraged me to the point where I could do whatever positive things I wanted in life through the powers of faith, focus and action.

These men inspire me today, but back in the '80s, I had no one to teach me how to hold a job and act responsibly. In fact, by the end of 1986, I had officially worn out my welcome at the F.B.I. My reputation was getting worse, and I felt like my supervisor talked to me as though I were a child. Steele continued to remind me that I was skating on really thin ice. He looked forward to one day rounding up the security guards and escorting me out of the building forever.

Although I had this monkey on my back named cocaine, I was still apt enough to apply to the Washington, D.C., police academy. With a high school diploma and a resumé that included a four-year stint at McDonald's as well as my time at the bureau, I was capable of landing a decent job. I did exactly that in April 1987 when I resigned from the bureau. I landed not just a mere job but a career in law enforcement after I completed a six-month tour as a Washington, D.C., police recruit.

I thought about wearing a uniform, gun and handcuffs and being a police officer one day. That really intrigued me. Perhaps I was looking for a career that demanded respect because I didn't fully respect myself. Perhaps I wanted to become a police officer because the field requires discipline, and I knew that was something I lacked in my life.

I joined the police academy in 1987 intending to follow the rigorous training and become Officer Stan Richards. My younger brother Cornell also made plans to become an officer. He graduated from the police academy in the previous class before mine. Perhaps hearing about Cornell's successful venture into law enforcement spurred my desire.

This was my second chance to prove that I belonged in the real world. I was no longer a high school teenager. I was a 26-year-old adult male in the prime of his life. I blamed my unsuccessful stint at the F.B.I. on Lamar Steele and the other racist supervisors who wanted to get me and placed no fault on myself.

For some crazy reason, I thought my dark secret [cocaine addiction] would suddenly vanish once I realized my interest in law enforcement, entered the police academy and became a peace [police] officer. I also concocted a plan.

After officially joining the academy, I decided to return straight home each day and not interact with anybody at night or on the weekends. I stopped socializing with my "usual suspects" [fellow drug users]. My entire life would consist of leaving home and going to the academy and vice versa. I wouldn't make any needless stops at the malls, nightclubs or even church on Sundays.

The police recruits had to adhere to a strict schedule: Monday through Friday from 7 a.m. to 3 p.m. Every morning after roll call, we ran three miles and exercised before class started. This was absolutely what I needed—a chance to get both my mind and body in tip-top shape.

Days turned into weeks and weeks turned into a month. I was doing great. I had gotten adjusted to my new schedule and way of life. Most important, I hadn't delved into any illegal narcotics. I had even taken a sabbatical from drinking alcohol.

In addition, I was making new friends and acquaintances at the police academy. These friends, I figured, would become lifetime acquaintances who would aid me in protecting and serving the people of Washington, D.C. I was on time every day and passed every test. After a while, I was completely at ease and let myself go.

I joked around and became sort of a class clown. After our daily run and before the class would officially start, I would go to the front, grab a microphone and make the entire class laugh by imitating some of our instructors. I really enjoyed my time as a police recruit. Man, our class [Class 87-1] had so much fun. We could have made another version of the 1984 movie, "Police Academy," that spawned six sequels mainly starring Steve Guttenberg, Bubba Smith and Michael Winslow.

During the early part of the summer, around June, I received my last check and retirement savings from the Federal Bureau of Investigations. The check was in the amount of $5,400. I thought that I was rich. I went out and immediately spent all of it on a 1984 gold convertible Corvette. This was rather convenient for me since my Toyota Supra would be disabled and totaled after undergoing the ordeal of an electrical fire.

I couldn't wait for Monday morning so I could show off my new car to the other recruits. Once again I would be Stan the man! I slipped back into old tendencies. I wanted to be the center of attention—or at least of my class. Some of the police academy instructors appeared envious or jealous of my new golden sports car. Rumors suddenly began to spread that I might be dealing drugs on the side. Many people believed back then that the only way an African-American could own an expensive car like a Mercedes Benz,

From the Bus to the Bentley

BMW, Cadillac or Corvette was to be a drug dealer.

Despite receiving that undesirable label, I loved the attention.

Ironically, I was actually clean and sober for the first time in many months. I hadn't used one ounce of cocaine in about 60 to 90 days. In those two to three months, I hardly appeared in public at night or on the weekends. I was ultra careful and terrified that I would mess up.

Around August, I started casually hanging out with some of my fellow recruits away from the academy. We would occasionally journey to the Classics nightclub on Allentown Road in Camp Springs, Maryland, on Thursday nights for happy hour. I would sip on some beer and alcohol, but never partook in any illicit drugs. I really thought that I had kicked my cocaine habit and had shaken the monkey off of my back.

Mitch Credle, a friend of mine since junior high school, also decided to join the police academy and coincidentally became a cadet in October 1986 with my brother Cornell.

"I was 22 years old at the time and I saw this advertisement in the newspaper about joining the police academy and becoming officers. I was a junior at the University of the District of Columbia [UDC] and had a four-year-old daughter at the time. Her mother was stressing me out about helping more with the bills since I only had a part-time job then. That's why I joined the force. It wasn't because I wished to become a cop or anything like that in school; far from it. It was out of necessity. Back then the starting salary was $22,500. It wasn't much but it was better than my part-time job," Credle said.

The now 24-year police veteran later completed his undergraduate degree in 1999. Credle has been a Metropolitan Police Department [MPD] homicide detective for 20 years.

"Stan and I were always really good friends but had different circles. We didn't hang out or party with each other, but when we saw each other at different events or functions, we hugged and talked like we saw each other every day. It was just a closeness, a connection," Credle once said, describing the nature of our life-long friendship.

"I have been at all of his major events in life including the Christmas parties and christenings. We always called him 'Stan the man' because of his skills on the basketball court, but off the court he was kind of laid back. People who didn't know him might have thought he was arrogant or something because he was light skinned and didn't talk much. During that era, people might have considered him a 'pretty boy.' That couldn't have been further from the truth," Credle claims.

The city's police academy was located in a somewhat isolated area of Southwest Washington called Blue Plains. The area was largely separated, for the most part, from residential and commercial establishments.

I kept up my routine for about five months. I was clean, sober and staying away from the terrible vices—liquor, marijuana, and most of all, cocaine. I can't say that the urges completely vanished, but I had another stronger focus in my life at that time. Officer Stan had such a nice ring to it. I just knew that law enforcement was my calling, my vocation, and that I would make a fine police officer one day.

Just like at the F.B.I., things went smoothly at first. My fellow recruits and I were approximately 30 days away from completing our academy training and becoming full-fledged Washington, D.C., police officers. I was ready to protect lives and property and serve mankind. In addition, I had been totally clean and sober for five months. I was living a natural high and I could envision the light at the end of the tunnel.

The month of September had just begun. The Labor Day Weekend was fast approaching. I remember our instructor warning us to have a good weekend but to remember that we were police officers first and foremost. He told us it was all right to party but basically we needed to conduct ourselves as model citizens. This was his way of hinting to abstain from alcohol [and needless to say] any illegal narcotics.

My fellow recruits and I also took the instructor's warning as a hint that there would probably be a drug [urine] test administered on the Tuesday following the three-day Labor Day weekend.

I decided to lock myself in the house for the entire three-day holiday weekend because I simply didn't trust myself. I did well all day Friday and Saturday. I didn't step a foot outside of my door. I vaguely remember watching plenty of television and listening to lots of music. Sunday morning and afternoon came and went as well. However, I got a call from my brother Tim Sunday evening inviting me to meet him at one of our favorite nightclubs, the Oak Tree in Oxon Hill, Maryland.

At first I said, "No way, no how!" I told Tim that my intentions were to study for my upcoming final examination at the police academy and then just relax.

By 10 p.m., however, I started convincing myself that it

would not hurt anything for me just to take a short ride to the club and check out my brother for a little while and hang out only in front of the club. Besides, I was sporting this convertible Corvette at the time and it would surely be an attention grabber.

It was a beautiful clear night. Perfect weather for a potential perfect storm! I arrived outside of the club around 11:30 p.m. and called Tim to come outside. He did and we casually started conversing.

"I only called him that night because in the past few months we had really not hung out or even got a chance to see each other. I just wanted to see my big brother. After all, we were always together and that long absence seemed like forever," Tim vividly recalls.

It was close to midnight and people were steadily entering the establishment, and the melodious music, although muffled, could be heard from outside. I began to get the urge to just listen to some music and do just a little partying. I convinced myself that I'd just go in to the club, but would do no drinking whatsoever.

After being in the club for no more than 10 or 15 minutes and seeing everybody partying and dancing—I lost it! I lost my composure. I lost my focus. I apparently lost both my mind and common sense.

I started by having a few drinks and later remember someone whispering in my ear that there was some good coke in the house, and it was on! Five months of sobriety ended just like that. At that point I could actually hear the cocaine calling my name and demanding that I partake. I was done—put a fork in me!

I bought a half gram for $50 and when that was finished [my appetite was huge because I hadn't indulged for almost half a year] went back and bought a gram for $100. By the time I left the Oak Tree early that Labor Day morning, I was as high as a kite. I was totally trashed! When I got home, I distinctly recall dropping to my knees and praying. I asked God why I had done what I did and jeopardized my career and five hard months of work.

When I woke up that Monday morning, my only concern was how to get that cocaine out of my system. I was sick to my stomach with worry and just plain sick to my stomach with the dope that I had snorted.

Somebody had once told me that if you drink white vinegar after using cocaine, it would clear your system and the drug would be undetectable in a urine test. So that's exactly what I did: consumed a bottle of white vinegar and then, for good measure, decided to run five miles for some exercise. Too bad I didn't decide to run the five miles instead of going to the club!

Tuesday morning arrived and I entered the academy right after roll call. The previous 24 hours since leaving the Oxon Hill nightclub were nothing but torture for me. I prayed and tried to bargain with God, saying that if He got me out of this I would never use drugs again. Everyone in my class was there milling about and discussing their weekend. I kept mum. Then it happened. Our instructor shouted the order, "Everyone to the clinic now."

We all headed down to the police academy clinic for our drug and urine test. I was very nervous. Why would anybody do what I had done and put an entire career in jeopardy? This test could and probably would decide my fate in regard to my law enforcement career. All the recruits headed back to the classroom at the academy after the drug test. They appeared to feel at ease. The day seemed like business as usual.

I, of course, could only think about the drug test and what my results might yield. I was a nervous wreck. Normally if someone tests positive for narcotics or a foreign substance, the results are released within 24 hours. By Thursday morning it had been more than 48 hours. I started to feel relief. The white vinegar must have done the trick. I started feeling lucky and believed that I had actually dodged a bullet.

On Friday morning my classmates and I were in the gymnasium preparing for physical training. Then I heard the instructor yell out another order. This time it wasn't for the whole class. It was simply for me.

"Richards...change up and go see Lieutenant Pittman."

That was the beginning of the end for me with the academy and the District police department. After having an extensive and thorough interview with the lieutenant, I was escorted downtown to the Internal Affairs office by a Sergeant Shaw.

Man! That must have been the longest ride of my life! It was unbearable. It was uncomfortable. It was simply humiliating. At the Internal Affairs office, I officially learned that I had failed my drug test. The academy found traces of cocaine in my urine. As is standard procedure, I went on administrative leave with pay while they conducted an investigation. I had to immediately surrender my gun and badge, and they escorted me home to retrieve all my uniforms and police gear. Finally, they escorted me back to my locker at the police academy so I could clean that out as well.

The procedure at the police academy was in place for recruits like me. I wasn't the first recruit to ever test positive for drugs and, unfortunately, I wouldn't be the last. Although I wasn't ready to bestow any compliments then, I must say that everyone treated me very fairly and with respect. Within the police department, most of the brass handle their difficult and often thankless jobs with professionalism and poise.

News about my administrative leave began spreading like wildfire. Rumors started that I had tested positive for narcotics and particularly cocaine. I remember two of my female classmates crying on my behalf as I cleaned out my locker and looking on disbelief because I appeared to be a clean-cut, well-groomed recruit who still had more than a streak of shyness to him.

Of course I swore that I was innocent and the test results were wrong. I denied it to the bitter end and even remember saying a couple of times that they must have switched my test results with someone else and that I'd return soon to the academy.
I knew that wasn't true. I could kiss the dream of being a Washington, D.C. police officer goodbye! Most of my friends and fellow recruits couldn't believe the rumors and allegations against me because I presented myself as a nice, clean-cut guy.

This had to be the worst and lowest point in my life—bar none! I had hit rock bottom! My shame and embarrassment transcended me and affected other members of the family. My little brother, Cornell Richards, had just graduated from the academy about six months earlier, and I knew my dismissal was going to hurt him too.

Using a baseball analogy to describe my life and current situation, this was strike two for me. I got strike one with the Federal Bureau of Investigations when I got a job with them straight out of high school. Now that I had cleared my locker out at the police academy, this was officially strike two. I had one more chance before I struck out!

From the Bus to the Bentley

Chapter 7

A good thing always happens when I get to a low point. I go into survival mode. I was on paid administrative leave with the Metropolitan Police Department [MPD] pending my investigation for failing my drug test. I knew the possibility of the department reversing its decision and bringing me back was 99.9 percent unlikely. But I still had my overall strength and good health. I also had determination and drive.

It was October and I started pounding the pavement, looking earnestly for any job. Midway through October, I landed a part-time job with the United Parcel Service [UPS] delivering parcels. They were hiring and getting ready for the upcoming holiday season.

I received a certified letter informing me that the MPD had fired me, and I no longer would be on administrative leave with pay. My law enforcement career had officially ended before it actually commenced. I had mixed emotions ranging from anger, disappointment, anxiety and finally depression.

"I was sick to my stomach when I heard about Stan's test and his being escorted out of the police academy. That really hurt me. Although he never blamed me, I blamed myself," said my brother, Tim.

"I was the one who called him to come out that Sunday evening. If I had never made that call, Stan would have been a police officer now," Tim added. "That night was a turning point for all of us. I might have smoked and drank a little after that, but after that night, because of what happened to Stan, I stopped messing with the hard stuff [namely cocaine]."

My temporary, part-time UPS job ended on Christmas Eve. During those particular Christmas holidays, I didn't feel merry at all. Instead, I slipped into a deep depression. I felt that the Grinch, the fictional character created by Dr. Seuss, had come and stolen my holiday joy, and I had no idea how to retrieve it.

My life was one big question mark. It seemed, like the popular commercial at that time, that I had fallen and couldn't get up! I had no job. I was behind on my rent. I had an upcoming car note [$543] for my Corvette due at the beginning of the year and, if that wasn't bad enough, my childhood sweetheart Reese left me for good.

We might have had some turbulent periods, but when she did pick the final time to leave, it was at one of my lowest points. I guess being kicked out of the police academy was the last straw for Reese.

All my dreams and aspirations appeared to be vanishing or dying off one by one. Most of my friends and classmates from the academy wanted nothing to do with me. I had the plague as far as they were concerned. I might as well have been diagnosed with leprosy.

After failing to secure another meaningful full-time job, I swallowed my pride and returned to the J. Edgar Hoover Building to seek employment with the bureau again. Based upon my record with the company and probably what was in my personnel folder, the F.B.I. turned me down flat.

With no steady income and unable to continuously dodge my landlord, I asked Cornell and his wife, Solina, if I could crash with them temporarily while I got back on my feet and found a gig. They were kind enough to give me a room in their newly purchased house to use and call my own.

It was January 1988 and this was the opportunity I needed. After settling in with my brother, his wife and Yakina, their 3-year-old daughter, I would leave the house each morning applying for jobs and attempting to land interviews. The house was located on Evarts Street in Northeast Washington. I looked for a job everywhere by searching the newspapers for advertisements, following up on friends' leads and doing anything else that came to mind. I was indeed humbled!

"I was happy to help Stan, my oldest brother, during his low point," says Cornell. "He stayed with us for about one year. It was like payback. He always took care of me as the youngest brother. As a big brother, Stan always looked after [us]. I won best dressed in high school one year with his clothes."

Cornell, who now resides in Durham, North Carolina, credits some of his major life accomplishments to our family work ethics and proudly cites being the first member of the Richards family to ever own a house. Cornell purchased his first house at the tender age of 21. The entire family was proud of him.

"[Solina and] I bought our first home after my graduation from the police academy and working as an officer. That was the same house where Stan stayed with us in Northeast—just a few blocks away from one of the areas we grew up, the Brentwood section of the city.

"We [all the siblings but especially the three brothers] were all blessed with incredible work ethics. As a District police officer in the 1980s, I once worked 36 hours straight. When the timekeeper saw my timesheet, an investigation was launched. They wouldn't believe that anyone could possibly work 36 hours straight without sleeping. After it was proven that I had indeed done the double [and triple] shifts, they gave me a commendation and then later changed the rules ensuring that no other officer would be allowed to work that many hours straight again," Cornell said.

"Those work ethics came from our father," added Tim Richards. "He didn't leave us with much, but he knew how to work. When he died, he left more than 100 hours of annual and sick leave at his job."

Like my father and brothers, I eventually reaped the benefits of hard work and determination. I got a job as a security guard at the Washington Grand Hyatt Hotel. It wasn't a bad job, and I was happy to have it until I noticed a few of my old police academy classmates, now full-fledged officers, assigned to that area. They would sometimes come into the hotel to eat lunch or buy a snack. I was more than a little envious, with a bit of jealousy on the side. We didn't speak, but deep down I wanted that job back so bad!

El DeBarge sings about needing a second chance, which is the title of his 2010 compact disc, after serving a year at California State Prison for a 2008 vandalism and drug possession charge. The rhythm and blues crooner has been seeking, among other things, a second chance at redemption after being freed from the taint of his cocaine addiction and resuming his recording career.

"I was in a drug coma. I went to sleep for about 22 years. I was crying to God, 'Lord, please help me get off this'," DeBarge said in an October 2010 edition of Ebony magazine. "I didn't give up hope. Drugs just had me. When I came out of my addiction, when God saw fit to have me locked up in prison, that was really a rescue. He let me know right there in prison, 'I had you the whole time'."

We, DeBarge and I, have some similarities. We both come from large families, had fathers who beat our mothers, overcame drug addictions and are currently bringing light-skinned back as sexy! I, too, wanted a second chance at atonement. Little did I know that a second chance was coming sooner than I could imagine.

After leaving the F.B.I., I applied for more than one job. I realized somewhat that I was drawn to government or civil servant employment like law enforcement. Therefore, I applied to both the MPD and the Prince George's County [in Maryland] police academy.

I received a letter from the Prince George's County police academy in January 1989. The letter stated that I was selected for an interview to eventually become a police officer within the state of Maryland. Along with the initial interview was a required polygraph examination with basic questions ranging from professional to personal history.

One of the series of questions was about my employment salary, habits and history. I told the administrator of the polygraph test that I had left the F.B.I. and began working at the Washington

Grand Hyatt Hotel because I was interested in hotel management. I also lied and said that I had never used any illegal narcotics before in my life. Somehow, someway I passed both the interview as well as the polygraph test. Don't ask me how. I still have no clue. The next month, February [1989], I was sworn into the Prince George's County police academy. When I think about that moment, I just say, "Wow!"

What was I thinking? I must have been in complete denial. I actually thought with my history and background at the Federal Bureau of Investigations and the Metropolitan Police Department [District of Columbia police academy] that I was going to have a long and successful career as a police officer in neighboring Prince George's County. That was ludicrous thinking.

The first few weeks at the Maryland police academy were fine. Everything went well with no incidents. It was basically the same daily routine that I had become accustomed to at the Washington, D.C. police academy.

Then the inevitable happened. One of the Prince George's County officers who would frequent the police academy in the District and play basketball with some of the instructors and recruits was at the academy one day and immediately recognized me. I probably outscored him on the basketball court.

The jig was up! The officer reported me to his superiors as being one of the recruits who was dismissed from the District police academy after failing a drug and urine test. Once again I was pulled from an activity with the other cadets and ordered to report to a high ranking officer.

This time the officers in charge were not so sympathetic to

me. After a lengthy interview, mainly discussing my history with the Washington, D.C., academy, I was summarily discharged from the Prince George's County police academy. The Maryland law enforcement officials were pissed that I had beaten their system!

How could a one-time disgraced recruit like me pass their so-called extensive background checks, polygraph test and interview without a blemish? That was the million- dollar question that nobody could answer.

Once again I had been kicked out of a police academy and once again I had lost both credibility and employment. Undoubtedly, this was strike three! I was out of options, so I went crawling back on my hands and knees [not literally but so it felt] to the Washington Grand Hyatt and begged for my old security guard job.

From the Bus to the Bentley

Chapter 8

Luckily, I got my old job back. However, I wasn't feeling very fortunate! I was at a job that I despised despite the fact that it was a good one. I guess I always had the stigma that security guards were nothing more than glorified rental cops who didn't get the respect of real police officers. Perhaps a little of that is true. But I've come to realize that no matter the job, the person deserves respect regardless of the title he or she holds.

In addition to feeling sorry for myself about my employment, I wasn't thrilled about my living conditions. Although my brother and sister-in-law, Cornell and Solina, treated me well, I had a hard time adjusting to living in one room. After all, I had lived my entire life in a crowded home with six other siblings before moving out and getting my own place. I wanted to be master of my own space once again.

To make matters worse, I had horrendous credit! I was still driving my new and beautiful Corvette but was constantly looking over my shoulder to detect the repossession guy. I knew that the dealership was in search of the car because I hadn't made a car note payment in several months.

Because I also couldn't afford my apartment, and the dealer didn't have my brother's address, I got some extra time with my beloved sports car. I also changed jobs so frequently, it was hard for the "snatch man" to find me at work. I used the hotel parking lot and avoided street parking as much as possible.

But I couldn't hide from my emotions. I was still in a deep funk of depression. My schedule generally consisted of going to work and returning home to my private room. For the most part, I had dropped out of the club scene and had isolated myself from family and friends. I had become a real loner, which wasn't extremely hard given my naturally shy personality.

What I still wasn't completely ready to admit was my dependency on cocaine. This was still my one true constant in life. At one point I even tried snorting heroin. I also realized that using needles wasn't my modus operandi [M.O.].

I'm thankful to this day that I never experimented with crack cocaine, which is a derivative of the pure powder that I snorted nasally. All reports suggest that crack cocaine fiends [and heroin users for that matter] usually become more addicted to the drugs and are often more violent in nature.

With my depressed state, I could have been one of those young men who, full of rage and trained to handle weapons, become a real menace to society like so many of our hardcore youth living the thug life in and out of prisons. I'm not saying that every youth involved in criminal activity is high on crack cocaine or some other substance, but these drugs strongly encourage an already enraged mind to commit more unspeakable acts of violence against people in his family, neighborhood and community.

In my case, I was rarely in touch with my family members, including my mother, between the end of 1987 and 1988. I occa-

92

sionally went past momma's home to visit her [and perhaps let her know that I was still alive]. She knew that something was wrong with me, but I guess she could never bring herself to ask exactly what. Had she asked, I seriously doubt I would have had the courage to tell her that my main problem in life was this habit I had of spending money for a particular white powder and then snorting it [like a pig] up my nose.

I always knew my momma to be a prayer warrior who could and would attend a church service for hours on end. I just never realized that one day it would benefit me. During one of my visits to her house, momma asked me to attend a church revival with her at the Washington, D.C., Convention Center located in the heart of downtown. The preacher and scheduled headliner that evening was an outspoken minister by the name of Frederick K.C. Price.

I initially told her I wasn't interested, but [thank God] momma didn't take no for a final answer. Momma insisted that she needed a ride and asked me again to take her. My momma didn't ask for much, and remembering that she was my best friend in the world, I realized that I couldn't say no to her twice.

Thinking back on it now, it was by far the best decision I've ever made in my life.

Best known for his weekly television and radio show, Ever Increasing Faith, Price has been preaching about faith, healing and prosperity for approximately 30 years. His weekly broadcasts reach an estimated 15 million people. Price established the Crenshaw Christian Center, one of the first African-American mega churches in the country, in 1973. The California native is the founder of the Faithdome which was erected in 1989 and dedicated the following year. The Faithdome seats nearly 10,000 people.

Momma and I went to the revival at the fairly new Washington, D.C., Convention Center, which the city built in 1983. Less than 11 years later, the city would erect a larger, more accommodating convention center and the '83 facility would become a vast parking lot. Mayor Barry was responsible for much of the city's initial boom and construction progress.

Immediately upon entering the gigantic facility, which at that time was the fourth largest convention center in the country, I felt God's anointing power and spirit. I can only imagine that this is how the 12 disciples, minus Judas, felt after receiving the Holy Spirit.

For the first time that I could remember, I felt a weight lift off of my shoulders. The service with Dr. Frederick K.C. Price was so powerful and moving, I didn't want to leave that evening. I probably wanted to stay even longer than momma, who was accustomed to attending these spiritual revivals and spending multiple hours in prayer. I was totally engrossed.

"I never knew it was about drugs," says momma today. "I noticed that [Stan] was depressed and hurting. I knew that my son was very hurt about something. I thought it was about his failure in the police academy, but I didn't know that drugs were involved. I always instilled in him that a failure is someone who fails with no hope and that a winner cannot be a winner without accomplishing something that involves effort."

At the end of the lengthy service, I distinctly remember the minister requesting an altar call for all of those individuals who needed special and specific healing. Although hundreds of people, if not thousands, had attended the meeting, I felt like Dr. Price was talking directly to me.

I really didn't want to walk down in front of this huge crowd of people I didn't know and stand in front of the stage. I also knew that I had no choice if I ever really wanted to get this psychological monkey, which had now grown into a full-grown gorilla named cocaine, completely off my back. I decided at that moment to end my many years of drug addiction, which started with smoking an occasional marijuana joint in high school and eventually led to spending the majority of my expendable income on cocaine.

I went to the altar and stood facing Dr. Price and my back to the crowd. The anointing of God was so intense and fervent, you could have cut the atmosphere with a knife.

When the minister and healer laid hands on me by touching the top of my head, I went numb from my head to my foot. I felt scared initially, but I soon realized something divine and spiritual was occurring. My entire body and soul felt wholeheartedly washed and scrubbed from top to bottom. I believe that I received healing at that moment. My invisible shackles, which were perhaps twice as binding as any you can actually see and feel, were gone.

I had, for possibly the first time ever in my life, experienced firsthand the true power of God. When I finally got back to my seat, I began hugging my mother and thanking her over and over and over again for inviting me and insisting that I drive her. Momma always did have my back!

From that date in 1988, I never used cocaine or drugs again. I went cold turkey!

I felt like a new man and I wanted to go about proving it. It had been about six years since I began using cocaine and I was determined to put that in the past and get on with my life

I sought to become the best human being I could possibly be. I joined the Evangel Church in Washington, D.C., and soon thereafter got baptized.

I began to humble myself and look at life differently. I suddenly could imagine what imprisoned men must feel like upon returning to their old communities after serving their sentences. I felt like I had gained my release from "incarceration" and had reentered society. I sought to establish a new life outside of my own personal prison walls.

I started to own up to my behavior and take full responsibility for my mistakes and the pain I caused others. I no longer blamed everybody else for my misfortunes. I accepted my faults and flaws and bad decisions.

I also became thankful for all the many gifts that I had, starting with my life. I was 27 years old and still in my prime. Although I had been under a cloud called cocaine since my adulthood, I still had my overall health. I hadn't been incarcerated, shot or seriously injured like so many other long-time drug users. I had night sweats or drug dreams for about a year after I quit. All I did was isolate myself and pray fervently with my Bible.

Stan & Chereace
Dr. Frederick K. C. Price & his wife

From the Bus to the Bentley

Chapter 9

"One-track mind: It all started 12:01 was the time. My man, $100 and a one-track mind; tired of being broke; being broke ain't no joke. Contemplating, perpetuating selling coke. Then my eyes blink and I started to think about the career of Stinky Dink. It is time to go hard and develop a one-track mind. Ask God to be my guide and come to create the riggedy raw; the riggedy raw on this date April 10, 1-9-9-0… my man, $100 and a one-track mind."

Those were the words of John "Stinky Dink" Bowman on his hit song "One-Track Mind." Bowman now plays at various venues with Familiar Faces in and around Washington, D.C. "One-Track Mind" was a fusion of go-go and hip hop with a sample of Michael Jackson's "Human Nature." The now 20-year-old song described how I felt at the time.

I had a one-track mind. I was getting my life back together by working two full-time jobs. I was hustling in the legal sense. I walked the straight and narrow path. First I was working the 11 p.m. to 7 a.m. shift at the Grand Hyatt, and then I got another gig as a security officer at the Sheraton Hotel on Capitol Hill from 2:30 p.m. to 10:30 p.m.

It's funny how God brings people in your life for a reason, season, or a lifetime. One of my co-workers, Terry Wayne Millinder, would always minister to me while we worked the midnight security shift at the Grand Hyatt. We became like brothers in a sense. Terry also helped me get the job at the Sheraton on Capitol Hill. He would always inspire me to reflect on the goodness of God.

When we worked at the Sheraton, Terry would always go to the rooftop of the hotel on his break time and pray. He would say, "Stan, I'm going to the mountaintop to be with the Lord." He was an awesome family man and had a great love for the Lord. Today he is pastor Terry Wayne Millender of Victorious Life Church in Alexandria, Virginia, and founder of Gospel Invasions Worldwide/Success for Life Initiative (www.pastorterry.com). We stayed in touch with each other through the years and recently launched a business venture together.

Back then, of course, I focused on the business of getting my life in order. My day-to-day routine wasn't easy, but I felt an urgency and gave it the utmost importance.

I slowly began to save money and get my life back. Now that I was off drugs completely, I could concentrate on other things that I had neglected for too long—like restoring my credit rating, re-establishing friendships and relationships and making five- to 10-year plans like most mature adults.

A consumer credit agent advised me on how to save money and restore my credit as well as settle old debts. My credit rating was in tatters. I started to save and budget seriously and continuously for the first time in my life. I saved every dime that I could get my hands on. Although I had to basically start from the beginning, the overall process had begun. If I couldn't exactly see the light at the end of the tunnel, I could at least envision it.

I also started applying for better-paying jobs with larger benefit packages and potential for promotion. I applied to both the federal government as well as the local government for available positions. I also applied to the Washington Metropolitan Area Transit Authority [WMATA]. This tri-jurisdictional government agency provides rapid transit service [trains and buses] within the interstate area of the District of Columbia, Maryland and Virginia [DMV]. Besides coordinating rail and bus procedures, WMATA, along with a public-private partnership, commands the DC Circulator bus system. Both the train and bus operations are commonly referred as the Metro system.

Once again I decided to isolate myself and focus on the prize. This helped me avoid negative influences and acquaintances who might still use drugs. I could also renew my faith, regularly attend church services and develop my relationship with God. I kept a simple schedule: I worked my two jobs, went to church on Sundays and did very little else besides exercise and sleep.

This routine also allowed me to recoup the life savings that I had basically squandered on vices—drugs and alcohol. By not spending money on socializing, entertainment or even [a lot of] dating, my bank account grew and my debt ratio decreased.

Still an avid sports fanatic, I listened every Sunday night, from 6:30 p.m. to 7:00 p.m., to local sports reporter Robert "Glenn" Harris' radio show on FM-96.3 [Howard University's commercial radio station]. The name of the half-hour program was "Let's Talk Sports." Harris, an ex-baseball jock who once played for the Washington Black Sox, concentrated on the sports of the day both nationally and locally. Harris attended Howard University from 1970 to

1974 on a baseball scholarship and later graduated from the historically black college with a degree in physical and urban education.

In 1995, Harris received the "Glenn Brenner Award" for outstanding contributions to young people in the community at the Regional Emmy Awards. That same year he was inducted into Howard University's Athletic Hall of Fame. Always encouraging and uplifting, Harris really inspired me during a rough period in my life. His show helped me get from one week to the next.

On May 5, 1989, I was hired by WMATA and became a part-time Metro bus operator. Man, I was so-o-o excited. I will always remember that date. That day was like my resurrection from the dead!

If you were a person of color who had grown up in Washington, DC, and didn't have a college degree, you typically aspired to three elite jobs: the post office, MPD or the Metro system. I had tried my hand with the police department, both in the District and Prince George's County, to no avail. Now, luckily, God had blessed me with an opportunity to work for WMATA. This time around, however, I had an ace up my sleeve. I no longer was working with a monkey or gorilla on my back!

I had prepared for this opportunity, and when I resigned from the hotel I knew that I would never work in that capacity again. Getting that Metro job was a huge break for me, even if it was just part-time at first. If I did well during my probationary period, other positions and full-time shifts might arise.

By December 1990, I was offered [and I accepted] a full-time position as a Metro bus operator. Life was coming together for me. I immediately started to work as much overtime that was humanly possible. To accomplish my plan, I needed to save my money.

I moved out of Cornell and Solina's home and into an apartment of my own in 1991. I continued to pay off all of my debts and renew my credit. Now that I was focused on the prize and not on the dope, everything I did had a purpose. No longer was I spending hundreds of dollars a week on drugs or alcohol at the club. Still, although the apartment was nice, I wasn't satisfied.

I had started my savings with one thought in mind: becoming a homeowner and buying my first house. I achieved this goal in February 1992 with the purchase of my condominium in Temple Hills, Maryland. This wasn't my ultimate dream house, but a great starter home specifically for a person in my position. I was truly excited about my life, and probably for the first time ever, fondly anticipated the future. I had a good Metro job, a new home and [most important] I was living drug-free and a healthy lifestyle.

The world seemed to be my oyster. I was jubilant. I was energetic. I was hopeful. I felt this way because of my new-found lifestyle. I was listening to the word of God, associating with positive people and working my plan. I also felt lucky and blessed to have overcome my drug demons and received yet another chance in life.

I continued to be a workaholic, which was easy to do as I wasn't married with children. I was working hard then [with the overtime], so that I wouldn't have to work as hard 10 years later. I would work so many different shifts and participate in so much overtime, I sometimes slept at the bus depot. As a single guy with no outside obligations, I didn't have to answer to anybody.

What I did have was a driving passion to show all the nay-sayers [or haters as they are called now] that they were wrong about me. I wasn't a loser! I could stay focused. I had determination, and that determination would lead me to the finish line as a winner. You don't always have to cross the finish line first to prove that you're a champion. Just cross it and you become an automatic winner.

Metro Employee of the Quarter

From the Bus to the Bentley

Chapter 10

Now that I had turned 30 years old and had gotten my career and life in order, I started to feel like something else was missing. That something, I determined, was steady female companionship. Although I had never been a guy with a lot of girlfriends like my brother Tim, I kept an eye open for that one woman—my future main squeeze.

After closing on my condominium, I started socializing more and attending parties at cabarets. Cabarets were as popular as go-go music to the Washington, D.C., area at one time. At cabarets, a large group gathers for a party or celebration.

Most Washington, D.C. cabarets take place in halls and lodges, and the tickets for admission are often part of a fundraiser. Typically the cabarets cater to a slightly older, mature crowd that doesn't necessarily want to patronize the nightclubs. The cabaret host will usually provide the entertainment, either a live band or disc jockey. Sometimes the host also will provide food or have it available for purchase. Most of the time, cabaret patrons would bring their own drinks because the host wouldn't have a license to sell alcohol.

Concert promoters hosted cabarets because go-go artists typically couldn't perform at the nightclubs or so-called upscale in-

107

stitutions around the District of Columbia and the metropolitan area. Go-go sometimes seemed to have an unfounded discriminatory stigma attached to it and its clientele. Although unfortunate incidents happened at go-go events around the area, those occurrences were no worse than what happens at rock-n-roll or heavy metal events. Hip-hop promoters struggled with the same type of discrimination and stigmas. Night club owners would sometimes want to charge more for extra security when concert promoters attempted to host a function with a go-go band, particularly if Chuck Brown wasn't performing.

Lil' Benny, Chuck Brown, the godfather of go-go,
Stan & James Funk

While attending such cabarets, I began thinking about my old job at the Grand Hyatt and some of the special events that occurred there. I worked the hotel's midnight shift and would always be on hand to witness the huge corporate galas. Everything about those hotel affairs was classy and elegant. They were lavish, to say the least. I distinctly remember being intrigued with these regular hotel extravaganzas.

Most of these high-powered affairs were sponsored and hosted by Caucasians. Some of these sponsors and hosts might have resided in the Washington, D.C., metropolitan area, but most were out-of-town visitors here in the nation's capital just temporarily. Sometimes I would stand in the hotel lobby and daydream. How could someone, like me, a hometown native, host such a spectacular event?

The key to any successful venture is imagining your success before it even occurs. In my daydreams at the hotel, I imagined myself as the host of one of these fine affairs. Why not me? I could have hundreds of guests coming to an event at the hotel dressed like they came out of an Ebony or Jet [magazine] showcase.

I decided to stop daydreaming and start doing! I became an entrepreneur—a person who organizes and manages any enterprise, especially a business, usually with considerable initiative and risk. I started hosting cabaret functions around the metropolitan area specifically under the heading MPD and Metro Associates. I decided upon this name because that was the clientele I sought -- middle-class people who could afford tickets.

I immediately succeeded at promoting events and filling venues. I didn't earn much money, but I realized I could host a classy affair. Besides, I really developed a love for event planning and party promotion.

Still, I faced fierce competition, and preparing for an event required a significant amount of work. Booking acts that would entice a majority of people to spend their hard-earned dollars was always challenging. To succeed in this business, the top person [me in this case] would have to outlay several thousands of dollars with the hope of recouping the money and making a profit at the end of the affair.

Promoters faced several risks involved along the way. If you held an event during the winter and a major snowstorm occurred that either shut down the city or strongly discouraged party-goers, the promoter would end up paying for such an unforeseen occurrence. Promoters could take out insurance for the event, but that didn't always cover everything. In addition, the insurance usually wasn't cheap.

Trina McIntosh and I met at a cabaret affiliated with MPD. She was a pretty young lady who also happened to be a Washington, D.C., police officer. Trina was light-skinned with a cute face and nice figure. It appeared to be love at first sight between the two of us. After dancing and conversing throughout that first night, we were practically inseparable. She liked me and I was definitely feeling her! If we didn't have such demanding jobs, we probably would have stayed by each other's sides.

After months of hosting cabarets and competing with other promoters, I decided to approach my top three competitors and [like Marlon Brando in the original "Godfather"] "make them an offer they couldn't refuse." It was August 1992 and I urged the guys—

Chris Bailey, Steve Mathis and William Redman—to stop squabbling for scraps and unite as one group for all the riches. They readily agreed and before you knew it, a coalition was formed.

We pondered over the group's name and suddenly I shouted out, "Let's name the group Positive Black Men Coalition." My thought behind the name was the fact that there was a shortage of positive black men in the area, and this moniker would attract the ladies to our functions. Wherever the ladies went, the men would soon follow.

Both professionally and personally, I experienced rapid changes. Within two months of our initial meeting, Trina moved into my condominium. Soon thereafter, Trina and I started talking about marriage. We became engaged about three months after she moved in with me.

Within 18 months, we planned a very flamboyant 1994 wedding at my old stomping grounds, the Washington Grand Hyatt Hotel. The wedding, with at least 300 people and a half dozen bridesmaids and groomsmen in attendance, cost us approximately $40,000.

Perhaps wanting to flaunt my success, Trina and I purchased a single-family home in Clinton, Maryland. I got all the frills and extras the builder offered with the house. In fact, I got even more options in our house than those advertised in the model.

However, in my mind it was all worth it. I had showed the naysayers and the haters that I had made it back from the depths of depression and hell! I now had a good Metro job, a brand new home and a cute police officer to call my own.

Life should have been perfect -- but it wasn't! Although Trina and I seemed perfect together on the surface, we never should have gotten married. At the very least, we should have courted much longer. Although we initially liked each other and were attracted physically, we really didn't know each other intimately.

I still hadn't gotten proper closure to my traumatic past with both the Metropolitan Police Department and Prince George's County police academies. Trina knew about my unsuccessful attempts to join the law enforcement ranks but probably never realized that I was still an emotional wreck after those failed attempts.

In my subconscious, however, I so wanted to be connected with law enforcement that I married the first single and attractive female police officer with whom I came into contact.

It would have been easier and less expensive if I had gone and sought professional counseling immediately after being released from the Prince George's County police academy. However, at that moment, I was too busy self-medicating with cocaine to pay attention to my emotional needs and state of mind.

Although we initially spent plenty of time together, our personal schedules became hectic after a while. I worked long hours and a lot of overtime at Metro and Trina did the same at MPD. She was doing her thing and I was doing mine. One year after our nuptials, Trina and I separated and eventually got divorced altogether in May 1999.

I went back to partying with one exception—no illicit or illegal drugs. I had learned my lesson! An individual could go out to a night club, public event or any social affair and simply enjoy the natural atmosphere, mood and people's company without the added pressure of being high.

Meanwhile, the Positive Black Men's Coalition [PBMC]

started to distinguish itself from other promotion companies and become a brand name in the Washington, D.C., metropolitan area or DMV [the District, Maryland and Virginia] as some refer to it today. We booked prominent acts both locally and nationally. We provided a social environment where mature adults could mix, mingle and network while enjoying musicians and headliners in rhythm and blues, jazz, hip-hop and, of course, go-go. We chose the most upscale venues, including the National Press Club, the Washington Convention Center, the Odyssey Cruise Line, Hyatt Regency Crystal City and the Hilton Alexandria Mark Hotel to name just a few.

Although we planned and worked hard, however, we weren't making any real money. After paying the overhead for each production, my partners and I would basically recoup our investment at best. Most of the time we lost money because no one had taught us any business skills. All of our associates loved us. We were making money for the radio stations, insurance people, the hoteliers, the print and radio advertisers, the caterers, and disc jockeys — everybody but us.

After doing this for about three or four years, I called a meeting with the guys. They all conceded that we were working hard with very little profit to show for our efforts. The other three guys decided that we'd had a nice run, but it was time to dissolve the partnership. I disagreed. I was ready to go in another direction. I thought that we should start working smarter not harder. Therefore, I continued PBMC on my own with help from my brother Tim, whose background in the hospitality industry proved invaluable.

Vernon Bowlding, Jr. and Robert Walker, Jr. joined PBMC in 1995 and 1999, respectively. Besides both men being named af-

113

ter their fathers, they both share event planning and coordination in their backgrounds.

The last member of PBMC is my nephew Sam "Bone" Martin, Jr. Sam, who just joined in 2010, is my sister Michelle and my brother-in-law Sam Sr.'s son. He received his Bachelor's degree from Bowie State University where he majored in business management and minored in entrepreneurship. I'm mentoring Sam to take my place in the PBMC organization sooner than later. Additionally, Sam is the owner of Martin's Restaurant and Lounge located at 1919 9th Street, N.W.

Through PBMC, I have met most, if not all, of the local athletes in town from the Washington Wizards to the Washington Redskins. Additionally, I met and took a photo with legendary attorney Johnnie Cochran right after the famous Orenthal James [O.J.] "The Juice" Simpson case. I also met extraordinary entrepreneur and hip-hop mogul Russell Simmons and motivational speaker Mr. Les Brown.

I remember meeting Les Brown when he started working at Radio One (magic 102.3) as an on-air personality. I met him through my sister, Michelle Martin, who also worked at Radio One. Les was looking for some key players in the D.C. area to network with to do some motivational speaking. Michelle mentioned me because I had a large network with PBMC.

Michelle scheduled a time for me to meet with Les Brown. I felt so honored. I also was extremely nervous. I'll never forget when he and I met at Radio One on a Friday.

When I met Les, he stated that he'd heard a lot of good things about me and he wanted to cut a valuable deal. He was looking to partner with me to get him in front of my network and for me to promote some events with him in the D.C. area. In return, he would mentor me and teach me how to speak and build wealth.

I was so excited about the deal and the chance to work directly with world-renowned Les Brown. After meeting with him for about a hour, he scheduled another meeting with me the following Friday.

The following week, my fear of success kicked in. I talked myself right out of the opportunity. I started telling myself that I was just a local party promoter and I wasn't worthy to work with Les Brown. I wasn't educated enough to speak in front of people.

When that following Friday came, I skipped my meeting with Les Brown and went to work some overtime driving the Metro bus. I didn't even have the respect to call and say I wasn't coming.

Thinking back now, I believe I was scared -- not that I wouldn't succeed but that I actually would succeed. I think a lot of people are like I used to be, scared of success. A few months later, I ran into Les Brown at a concert and I will never forget that look he gave me. He just stared at me and shook his head. Boy, I felt like a big loser. Its funny how we miss out on opportunities every day simply because we don't take advantage of those moments and position ourselves around the right people.

I've made a lot of mistakes, and PBMC has had its share of challenges and rewards. No one ever taught me business. I started doing parties at hotels because of the sheer joy of it. We've been a part of making history in the DMV and we've put smiles on many faces along the way. However, it hasn't been all smooth sailing. The overhead continues to be a beast!

Stan with Les Brown

Stan with Johnnie Cochran

From the Bus to the Bentley

Chapter 11

Although PBMC enjoyed some success during the early years, I was a plain, old basket case after breaking up with Trina, my first wife. All I had in my life was work. That's all I ever did. I would attempt to go to church on Sundays too but that lasted for just a couple of hours. I would leave Metro and promote a PBMC affair and then leave that and go back and work some more. I was officially a workaholic.

It helps that I can get by with very little sleep. Statistics show that most Americans average about 7.5 hours of sleep within a 24-hour period. I could always get by with less. As a Metro bus driver, I averaged just four hours a day after doing overtime and double shifts.

I dated but not a whole lot. My track record with women wasn't spectacular. Reese was gone, and I was separated and soon-to-be divorced from my bride of just one year.

One time, after completing a shift on the No. 70 bus route that traveled up and down Georgia Avenue and crossed into Silver Spring, Maryland, I pulled off the road and vomited. I let it all out. I didn't have an upset stomach or virus. I was depressed about the women in my life -- or lack thereof -- and my pending divorce. All my siblings and close friends had found that special soul mate.

Where was mine?

Then it happened when I was least expecting it. I met some-one special. The Positive Black Men's Coalition planned to sponsor a Christmas party at the snazzy Southwest Washington nightclub and restaurant that was then called the Foxtrappe. The club, which is the last large one of its kind in that area, is now known as Zanzibar on the Waterfront.

Chereace Spriggs saw a flyer about the affair and beeped me for tickets. This was 1996 and we were still using beepers back then. When I delivered the tickets to her, my mouth popped open. Wow! I thought she was drop-dead gorgeous. By far, I found her to be the most attractive woman I had ever laid eyes on, but what could I do? As I mentioned before, I was a basket case because of my other failed relationships and particularly my pending divorce.

Chereace Antoinette Spriggs was born on August 6, 1970, to Harold and Lucy Spriggs in Washington, DC. Two years later, her parents gave birth to her only biological sister, Nicole Denise. Her parents would go on to divorce, and both later remarried other people.

"After my parents divorced, I grew up in the home with just my mom and my sister, Nicole. We lived in an apartment complex in Oxon Hill, Maryland. My dad would visit us regularly. One thing my mom never did was bad mouth my dad around us or try in any way to keep us away from him. I always respected her for that."

Describing her mom as the most unselfish person she knows, Chereace says her mother always catered to her two girls. "She took us shopping on the weekends and even ordered clothes for us from one of her favorite catalogs, Spiegel. Those experiences birthed my love of fashion."

Even as a child, Chereace always desired something more out of life. "I had dreams and visions for my life, and working a 9-to-5 for 30 to 40 years wasn't part of the vision. I can't tell you where those thoughts came from because my parents always worked a job. My dad had a career in the Air Force, so I didn't have examples of entreprenuership in the family. It was a seed inside of me. I always had big dreams."

Life was great for Chereace, her sister and her mom. The routine changed when Chereace's mom met Edwin in 1985 and married him in 1988. "He really was a nice man," Chereace says, "and would charm my sister and me by bringing snacks to our house when he would come to visit us."

Her mother's marriage to Edwin, however, meant moving to what seemed like the other end of town. Chereace had just started high school at Oxon Hill Senior High School, so she wasn't happy about changing schools. She realized, however, that she didn't have much choice. In the fall of 1985, she enrolled as a sophmore in Central Senior High School.

Always ambitious, Chereace excelled in academics consistenly and stayed on the honor roll. She also participated in such extracurricular activities as the the Pom-Pom squad and the modeling club (she hopcd to model when she grew up). She also was a member of the National Honor Society. Chereace graduated in the top 10 percent of her class with honors.

"Over the years, I've worked hard, studied long, applied myself and changed courses if necessary to win," she says. "These are characteristics that I exhibited as a child and ones that have carried me today. I firmly believe that hard work always pays off."

During her senior year, Chereace prepared for college with her mom. She ultimately chose to attend the University of Maryland Eastern Shore.

"I will never forget taking that three-hour drive to Princess Anne, Maryland, with my mom. I got settled into my dorm room and met my roommate, who was from Chicago. Then it was time for my mom to leave. I still remember to this day watching her walk off into the distance. I was scared, but at the same time I was ready."

Chereace entered a world of freedom and choice without parental supervision. She could set her own schedule -- which could mean finishing classes by early afternoon and having Fridays off or spending time watching Oprah and soap operas. Parties and football games took place every weekend.

"I had to discipline myself to study and not give in to all the distractions and temptations," she says today. " My first semester grades were not as I'd hoped. My grade point average was below 3.0, which was highly uncharacteristic for me. That experience was a reality check."

Chereace saw her grades improve during the second semester as she learned to balance life as a college freshman. "The life lesson: I could have it all, just not all at once," she says. "College challenged me, but I've always been willing to try new things. I guess that was the ambitious part of me trying to come out, but I suppressed it until much later in life. God gives us glimpses of who we are but we often ignore Him, perhaps out of fear or unbelief.

Whatever the case, I didn't fully realize my strength in Him until much later in life."

Chereace would go on to be the second person in her family to graduate from college. Her now-deceased Uncle Thad, who was her mother's brother, was the first. "I highly recommend college, and especially going away to college if that's possible. That's where you can learn lessons that prepare you for the tough world that's waiting for you. I encourage young people to absorb all that the college experience has to offer. They should focus not only on just the academics, but they also should get involved in the extracurricular activities and meet new friends. These relationships can last a lifetime and provide valuable leads and business opportunities once you begin your professional career."

After graduating again with honors and receiving a bachelor's of science degree in computer science, Chereace sought full-time employment in corporate America. Her first job was as a help desk technician for the Hopkins & Sutter law firm.

"Shortly after starting my job, I would move from my mom and stepdad's home because my stepdad wanted me to pay $300 for rent," Chereace recalls. I thought that was absurd as I was just getting established in the "real world." I would have agreed to pay $100, $200 tops, but $300 was just out of the question. So I left. I moved in with my dad, and, boy, did I enter the "real world."

For the next few years she had no direction or real sense of purpose in her personal life. She met Jeffrey Gailliard and married him in November 1994.

"Looking back, that was one of the craziest things I ever did, and I knew it immediately," Chereace says. "We never had a great relationship. Jeff was federal worker. I, on the other hand, was a young, ambitious young woman on a mission to excel in corporate America. The two personalities didn't mix well at all. Within a year and a half, I was a wreck and couldn't take the relationship any longer."

The turning point for Chereace came when she attended a church service with one of her girlfriends. During the altar call she gave her life to Christ. "I was at the end of my rope mentally and sought help from the only source I could count on -- Jesus. That day felt weird but great. I felt I had a new lease on life."

Chereace found the courage to leave Jeff and begin working on herself. She moved in with her grandmother and grandfather and slept on a sofabed in their den. "I totally relied on the Lord for my strength," says Chereace "It was still a very difficult decision to leave my marriage, and after I left, I began to seek hard after God for guidance and direction." She joined Ebenezer African Methodist Episcopal Church and became active in the Young Adult Ministry. She attended church and Bible study regularly and prayed often.

Chereace still excelled in corporate America, and by 1996 she was earning a good salary, especially considering that she'd just entered the workforce two years earlier. Because she had more free time, she decided to get a second job at Hecht's -- now known as Macy's -- in Tyson's Corner Mall, which was located near her full-time job.

With her professional life intact, Chereace began to develop a relationship with herself. "I would hang out by myself, go to the movies and go out to eat," she says. "I was doing something I had never done before, spending quality time with me. I was determined to be whole and complete. To know who I was, what I like, and what type of man I would want. A man who wouldn't complete me but enhance me. I didn't date at all because I was focused on my relationship with God and myself. I didn't want a relationship until I knew I could make myself happy and complete."

During this time of self-examination, Chereace occasionally traveled for her job. "I remember going to Orlando, Florida, for the first time. I was on business and did the occasional dinner with co-workers. But one day I had the entire day to myself. I remember strolling alone along the boardwalk and having the best time. Chereace and I bonded, and we had a wonderful time together. I went to the movies and a seafood restaurant, where I fully enjoyed the seafood buffet.

"That was a major moment in my life. I had built an intimate relationship with the Lord and learned to hear His voice, and I had built this amazing relationship with myself. Soon after, I felt God had given me the space not to go back to my marriage, and I informed Jeff. This was in 2006.

"I had totally forgiven Jeff for all that he took me through, realizing that I attracted a mirror reflection of who I was. I held no hard feelings for him and really encouraged him to seek professional counseling for healing. I never expected that getting tickets to a cabaret would be a turning point in my life."

From the Bus to the Bentley

PART III

From the Bus to the Bentley

Chapter 12

"I had never heard of the Positive Black Men's Coalition before that Christmas event, but I wanted to see the artist [headlining the affair]—Howard Hewitt," the former Ms. Spriggs says.
"I made sure I was wearing a nice outfit because this guy was supposed to stop by my job so that I could buy these tickets for the concert. I had these wide leg jeans on with a matching print shirt and vest. Stan came by, introduced himself and repeated his standard and formal line: 'Thank you for supporting us, enjoy yourself, and I look forward to seeing you at the event.' I remember thinking he was a nice-looking guy."

After that 1996 Christmas party at the Foxtrappe that featured former Shalamar lead singer and balladeer Howard Hewitt, I didn't expect to see Chereace again. We hadn't exchanged telephone numbers, and although I knew she worked at the Department of Transportation, I couldn't go back there and just hang out each day hoping for a glimpse of her.

Luckily, my PBMC partner Chris Bailey remembered seeing her at his job. Although it [the Department of Transportation] was a large federal building, Chris would sometimes see Chereace in the cafeteria. I remember asking Chris during our PMBC meeting if he had seen that beautiful girl named Chereace anymore at work. I went on to mention to him and my partners that if I ever got to see her again, she would be mine.

Chereace and her girlfriends had so much fun at the Christmas affair, they ventured to a second PBMC affair in either March or April of 1997. This time I made up my mind to approach her and strike up a conversation. What's your status, I vividly recalled asking her. Chereace told me she was single although in actuality she was separated from her spouse like me. That was our common starting ground: We were both a couple of basket cases!

We exchanged information that time, and I began having long, enjoyable telephone conversations with her practically every day while she was on her job. I would be talking from home because I was on the night shift [4 p.m. to midnight] then for Metro. "Because I lived at home in my grandmother's house [on Capitol Hill] and Stan lived in his Temple Hills condo with his sister at the time, we were careful and really did nothing but date outside," Chereace says.

"I clearly remember Stan picking me up from work at lunch once in his shiny new BMW with the chrome rims and everything" she added. "We were going out on our first date. He was really proud of that car, and he really looked good in it."

Man, that was the best date of my life! I was so nervous but cool at the same time. She was so beautiful, and I just wanted to be in her presence. I picked her up at noon at the Department of Transportation on 7th and D Streets in Northwest Washington. I was most definitely on time. I got out and opened her door. It was a beautiful, sunny day. We went to the Market Inn for lunch. I remember asking her if I could hold her hands while I blessed the food. After an awesome lunch, I took her back to work. I opened her door again, shook her hand and thanked her for spending time with me.

After that, it was on and poppin.' We couldn't get enough of each other. We would see each other every day, and when we weren't together we were on the phone. Thinking back now, it was an awesome courtship. I recall meeting her family for the first time. Her mom Lucy and I hit it off the first time we met. Her stepdad Edwin was a different story. He played hard ball for about six months, but after a little wining and dining I had him in the palm of my hand.

Our courtship began as friends, and we enjoyed spending time together. "We got along on many different levels. Our values and beliefs were in sync and we agreed on things like marriage, kids, family, and money," remembers Chereace.

"I must admit it wasn't really love at first sight but we had a connection once we began talking," she added. "We would talk for hours and hours about everything. We learned that we both were experiencing the same thing in our marriages. It was as if our worlds collided at the perfect time. We became each other's confidant and true friend. We even counseled each other on our marriages. Even though we felt this instant connection, we took our relationship extremely slow because neither one of us had complete closure on our existing relationships."

Still, our relationship quickly blossomed. "I just instantly felt free with Stan," says Chereace. "I thoroughly enjoyed EVERY minute with him. I didn't care if it was on the phone or in person I just wanted to be connected to him. From 1997 to 1999, we became inseparable. Although he worked long hours and I worked both my full-time and part-time jobs, we always made time for each other. We did everything together. In the summer of 1997, we fell in love."

Chereace planned to attend the annual New Orleans Music Festival with her girlfriends during the 4th of July weekend in 1997. I decided to attend with my friends. Even though we went there separately, we were inseparable the entire weekend.

Uncle Hollis, Glynda, Stan, Chereace, Glynis Brown, Steve Mathis
Vernon & Tim in 1997

"We had a ball spending time with each other, much to our group's dismay," says Chereace. "After all, we hadn't planned to go together. It was during this trip that we fell in love, strolling down Bourbon Street hand in hand. I knew in my heart that this was the man for me and that we would be together forever. On the plane ride home, Stan wrote me a note that I still have to this day. It said, Some how, Some day, Some way, Me and You, which was dated July 4, 1997."

Stan & Chereace having a ball in New Orleans

I believe Chereace and I both knew fairly early in our relationship that we had met our soul mate but we had to get closure on our marriages. In 1998, we decided to give our marriages one last try. We didn't want our relationship to be a rebound and later have regrets.

I remember moving back into my house with Trina, but after a few weeks it just wasn't happening. I remember saying to myself, "Stan make a decision and live and die with that decision." So I decided to leave for good. I believe most people never move forward in life because they just don't make decisions.

Once we got closure with our marriages, our relationship really kicked up a notch. We did everything together from hanging out to traveling. We really became best friends. Because Chereace was a corporate girl, she would travel the country a lot and let me tag along. Keep in mind I was a blue-collar worker and never traveled. She would do corporate speaking conferences all the time.

I recall once we were in Las Vegas at the beautiful Belaggio hotel, where Chereace planned to speak during a seminar. I came down from our room because I wanted to see her in action. Man, it was big business. I witnessed about 1,000 businessmen and woman moving and shaking at the conference.

I started to experience mixed emotions. I was proud of her but at the same time I was hatin' on her because I was a blue-collar worker, a bus operator. We had our meetings in the employee lounge at the bus garage. Deep down, I wanted a part of her world. I must say, though, that my queen never treated me like I was different.

Her divorce came up quicker than mine because she and her husband didn't have any property together or credit cards in each other's names like Trina and I did. Chereace was officially divorced in August 1998, and mine came about nine months later. Isn't it interesting how you can elope and get married in a day, but it takes months and years to get separated or divorced? I guess that's why God designed marriage to last forever.

I believe God brought Chereace to me to resurrect my love. We both have so much in common. We both love the Lord and are God-fearing people. We both are very secure with who we are as

Welcome To
Social S
Com

Your Num

N 2 5

lease take a seat until your
ber is called.

lete a paper application
rovide required documents.

7/11/2012 2:01:48 PM

Welcome T

ease take a seat until your
ber is called.

lete a paper application.
rovide required documents.

7/11/2012 2:01:48 PM

people, even though Chereace is nearly 10 years [nine years, three months] my junior.

While in the police academy I fell in love with running long distance. Chereace and I would go on dates to the park and I would run about 3 miles while she would walk. Finally, I got her to run for a minute then walk a minute. After doing this for a while, she got what we call the "runner's high" and fell in love with running as well.

"We loved running so much, we decided to enroll and train for a marathon," says Chereace. The marathon training regimen ca'ꞁꞁ for a weekly "long" run every Saturday morning, along with tw weekly runs for six months. In October 1999, we ran and completed the 24th Annual Marine Corps Marathon together. Actually, I crossed the finish line 10 minutes ahead of him.

Stan & Chereace at the end
of the 1999 Marine Corps Marathon

I proposed to her in 1999 after we had finished running 26.2 miles at the marathon. The actual proposal didn't take place at the finish line in front of a bunch of strangers, but rather inside our private Doubletree Hotel room in Crystal City, Virginia. When I met her family and saw that they were good people, I knew she would be my wife. Thus, ended a great courtship!

Our engagement!

Celebrating the marathon and our
engagement

We were married a year later on August 18, 2000. After our wedding, we spent the next 11 days in Hawaii enjoying our honeymoon. "Three months after we were married, I conceived my first child -- a son born July 12, 2001 -- whom we named Stanley Garnell Richards, Jr.," says Chereace. Four years later we had another son, born November 16, 2005, Isaiah Matthew.

My family, the reasons WHY I do what I do.
Stan, Jr., Stan, Sr., Chereace & Isaiah

We had a normal life, great jobs, wonderful kids, a nice home, cars and all the niceties that come along when there are two working adults in the home. "Stan worked crazy hours to make six figures per year, and my corporate job paid me almost as much annually," says Chereace. "We had the "stuff" but no time."

My childhood dreams of wanting a wife, family and house with the white picket fence had finally come to fruition. When my oldest boy, Stanley Garnell Richards, Jr., was born in 2001, it definitely was icing on the cake. Four years later, his brother, Isaiah, became the latest member of our household. My wife and two sons are my pride and joy.

The first five years of our marriage were good but something was missing: time. By 2005, we were like two ships passing in the middle of the night. I was working a lot over overtime (80-100 hours a week) to maintain my lifestyle. We had bought a bigger

Cornell, Stan & Tim

house, and with that came more bills. I felt that as the man of the house, I had to make things happen for my family, so I was living on the job. I was beginning to lose my joy because of the lack of time with my family. Stan Jr. once asked me, "Dad when are you ever off from work?"

The straw that broke the camel's back was in May of 2005 when my brother Cornell almost died from a major surgery. Then in December, my brother Tim was diagnosed with pancreatic cancer. I remember getting in the mirror on New Year's Eve in December 2005 and taking a good look at the way I was living. Here I was working 80-100 hours a week living on the job back in the hood where I came from. I had a nice home and cars, but at the end of the day I didn't have time with my beautiful family. Was this real success?

On January 2006 I made a promise to myself and Chereace that I wasn't going to work anymore overtime. I remember praying and asking God to send something my way. I was in way over my head with the new house and cars.

For Chereace, life took an unexpected twist in 2002. "That was the day my boss flew in from Atlanta, called me into the conference room and, with HR on the telephone, informed me that would be my last day with the company. I'll never forget the emotions I felt as they proceeded to give me details--the sadness, the sense of failure. How would I tell people? What would they think about me?"

That painful decision actually served as the push she needed to reach her destiny. "Truth be told, we get complacent with a job and a paycheck and all the stuff that comes along with it," says Chereace. "And then we end up with more month than you have money. I know because I've been there! Looking like a million bucks and in reality barely having enough money to buy lunch. I call it being broke but on a higher level."

That decision prompted Chereace to change her mindset, pursue something of her own and start a business. "I just needed to find the right business....the right opportunity," she says.

After reflecting on what she'd wanted as a child, the lifestyle that she'd dreamed about while growing up, Chereace began researching businesses she could start. After my research, however, I realized that I would need a lot of money and time to start a "traditional" type of business, neither of which I had. So I waited.

A few months after her layoff, Chereace got a "stable" job in the federal government. "I was so excited because now I would have a good job, with benefits," she says. "In my mind, I thought this was a good way to protect myself from another layoff. The federal government would be a safe place for me to plant my flag, grow professionally and retire. In retrospect, at this point I was definitely complacent because I never wanted to experience a layoff again. I had a family and couldn't stand the financial devastation."

This job proved to be rewarding as Chereace won a promotion to a manager's position with a salary that exceeded what she'd earned in corporate America. "I was accumulating leave, had a coveted garage parking space, and now called the shots," she said. "I set my sights on advancing further into the Senior Executive Service (SES) ranks. In my mind, I was going to go places in the federal government because I was never one to be content. I was always reaching and moving ahead."

She went on to get a master's degree in information technology management from American University in 2005.

But even though she felt content from a job security standpoint, she still had the urge to pursue her dream of starting a business. "My income was great," she says, "but I wasn't fulfilled."

From the Bus to the Bentley

Chapter 13

Then the 5LINX opportunity showed up in May 2006.
"God is amazing, and His timing is always right," says Chereace.
"Just a few years prior, Stan and I were so against network marketing. I was a little hesitant now simply because I'd never done anything like this before, but I was ready for something different!"

My nephew introduced us to the business only because he wanted to use our basement to launch his new venture. Chereace and I begrudgingly agreed to let Sam, my nephew and PBMC partner, have his affair in our basement on one condition: The event needed to be over by 8:00 p.m. because we planned to host a fight party that same night. "Had he invited us out, we would have never attended," says Chereace. "But, since the meeting was in our home, we watched the presentation."

Sam had invited a few close friends and associates to our home to hear Tishina Pettiford, an Executive Director with 5LINX at that time, address them about a new potential financial opportunity. He didn't ask me or Chereace to participate. I guess he thought that we would never consider the direct sales industry or multi-level marketing.

"I really wanted to ask him to be a part of the meeting but I was kind of scared that he wouldn't be interested," states Sam, 33, who was already linked with the organization. "After only 11 or 12 people showed up that night, [Stan] came downstairs to lend some support and began listening to the presentation from the back of the room. About 10 or 15 minutes later, Chereace came down, and the rest is history."

When I saw the technology, I was immediately intrigued. I was always skeptical [about people asking for money] but something about the 5LINX technology motivated me.

Recalls Chereace: "I was impressed by the fact that with 5LINX, I could get paid on bills I was using all ready. In my mind, it just made sense. Even though, I didn't really understand the concept, I was excited about the idea of getting paid on bills I was already paying."

Out of about 13 people in my basement, I was the only one to get started. I knew that the 5LINX video phone would only get better as technology evolved. At the end of the presentation, Tishina Pettiford asked if anyone saw an opportunity with 5LINX. I said, yes, and was the only one to get started. Because it was so close to the time for my fight party to start, I asked her to come back the very next Saturday to do a meeting for me.

The next Saturday, May 14th, Chereace and I launched a brand new 5LINX home-based business. From that point, our lives changed forever.

Chereace says, "I knew 5LINX made sense, I just didn't realize it would and could do all of what it has done for us: retire me and my husband within two years, send us to the top position in the comp plan, allow us to buy houses and cars for family members. This opportunity has blessed us to be in a position to be a blessing to the people we love the most."

Tishina introduced us to 5LINX National Director, at the time, Lisa Cloud. With her mentorship, Chereace and I started building the 5LINX opportunity in Maryland. After a few weeks in the business, Chereace and I flew out to Los Angeles to meet Senior Vice Presidents, at the time, Barry Donalson and C. Anthony Harris. These two industry experts, along with Lisa and Tishina, exposed us to a different life.

Barry Donalson is an industry icon and someone I respect tremendously. His direct, in-your-face style is one I sought to imitate. I wanted to command a room as he did every time I stepped up front. I learned confidence and boldness from Mr. Donalson.

I connected with C. Anthony Harris' gentle spirit. Mr. Harris has a kind spirit and a desire to help other people. Growing up in the industry, I would always say I wanted to be bold like Barry in front of the room and gentle like C. Anthony every day.

From Lisa Cloud, I learned how to be a student of the industry. She modeled continuous learning, and I wanted to learn my craft as she demonstrated. Lisa mentored me and Chereace all the way to the Senior Vice President level and taught us a proven system for success. Tishina Pettiford was like a sister to us. At 27, she was ambitious and driven. We bonded quickly and learned this business together.

We quickly learned there was a world out there to which we hadn't been exposed. We didn't know people made more money in a month than most people made in a year. This world of free enterprise is a world where you can create what you want and be all that you want to be. This new world provided opportunities for us to travel, meet great people and help others create the life they want through this vehicle. 5LINX is a vehicle that can move people from where they are to where they want to be personally, spiritually, and professionally. It's all about making a decision to change your current circumstances.

Today, I think a lot of people are starting to embrace the direct sales industry because corporate America and the economy are failing the masses big time.

The history of 5LINX dates back to 2001 when the three co-founders -- Jason Guck, Craig Jerabeck and Jeb Tyler -- formed a partnership in Rochester, New York. CEO and President Jerabeck's initial idea was to launch an Internet-based business, but Guck and Tyler persuaded him to form a network marketing enterprise instead. Jerabeck noted that the company derived its name from five principles: vision, integrity, opportunity, freedom and success.

The company's foundation is a telecommunications service that comprises digital phone service, wireless phones, telephone accessories [with calling plans] and broadband Internet service. 5LINX's flagship product is the exclusive state-of-the-art videophone that allows users to see as well as hear the people they call. The company recently launched 5LINX Energy (gas and electric). What excites me about this company is the fact that it stays on the cutting edge of the latest technology.

In addition, 5LINX began introducing other home services such as satellite television, home security systems and identity theft protection. The enterprise acts as a broker for other Fortune 500 companies such as Verizon, Sprint, T-Mobile and Dish Network.

The direct-sales business, also known as network marketing,

is one of the most negatively stereotyped industries. I personally can attest to that as I was against the industry of network marketing prior to getting started with 5LINX. Admittedly, I didn't know enough about the industry to come to an educated conclusion. I bought into all of the negative stories I heard about the industry, most commonly that it was a "pyramid scheme." For the record, "pyramids" are illegal as they typically don't involve real products or services.

Upon extensive research, I learned that anyone can be successful in this industry. You don't have to get a degree, acquire certifications or go to school. I've come to realize that as long as you possess a desire and willingness to change, as well as the will to stay the course, you can succeed in this industry. More millionaires have been created from this industry than any other I know of. Most of the success stories come from people who had very humble beginnings, like me.

One of my "whys" -- my reason for getting and staying involved with 5LINX -- was time with family. The first two business partners I got for 5LINX were my brothers Cornell and Timothy in that order.

Tim, who was always my sandbox pal and closest sibling, had learned in December 2005 that he suffered with pancreatic cancer. When we [the family] learned of his condition, it changed our lives. I decided that I would face all my fears in life. I decided to spend more time with my wife and sons. I decided to speak the truth and use my life as a symbol for others. 5LINX came along and cemented this decision.

"I'm not supposed to be alive right now. The doctor gave me

four to five months to live in 2005, but through the power of God here I am five years later," Tim testifies today.

"I've had more than 31 surgeries in my life. I have terminal cancer. One day I will lose this battle," adds my brother, the 47-year-old miracle patient who retired from the hospitality field on disability.

"I was suffering for months with this terrible pain in my chest and abdomen," says Tim. "I was misdiagnosed several times by my regular doctor supplied by my company's HMO plan.
"Finally, my wife took me to Dr. Habib Farhoudi, who practices internal medicine in Silver Spring, Maryland. He sent me to the Clinton Imaging facility where it was determined, correctly, that I had a tumor outside of my liver. I had liver surgery in 2006."

That led to my brother Tim finding an incomparable team of physicians at Johns Hopkins Hospital led by Dr. John L. Cameron. "If not for Dr. Cameron, I wouldn't be here now," Tim says.

Jason Guck, Stan & Craig Jerabeck
after a 5LINX National Convention

Tim is my daily motivation. Any day that I feel tired or sick and question if I want to give a presentation or work, I think about Tim and refocus. His attitude and spirit inspire me.

Although Tim's illness increased my desire to spend more time with my family and pursue my dreams, what really drove me in 5LINX was when my friends ran away from me. Then I had something to prove. I couldn't believe that my so-called business minded friends wouldn't even take a look at the business. It made me realize the type of people I had in my circle.

I've heard that we're the sum total of the five people in our circle. If you want to go to the next level in life, you have to position yourself around people who have what you want.

I've also learned that you're only as good as your network. I realized that I was stuck where I was simply because of the people I hung around. Some of the guys at the bus garage, love them as I do, grew complacent. But I had dreams. I wanted to go places. The lifestyle I wanted just wasn't going to happen if I stayed where I was around the people I was spending a lot of time with. I wanted to be a millionaire, and before 5LINX I didn't know any. So I had to position myself around different people, people like Barry Donalson, C. Anthony Harris and the co-founders of 5LINX.

Despite the adverse reaction I received from many of my associates and friends, I still cornered each and every one of them and explained the 5LINX concept to them. Within a month, Chereace and I had recruited 20 people to the organization. We were progressing nicely, and we could see this business had potential if we continued.

One of my biggest fears at that time was getting up in front of people to speak. I didn't think I was qualified to do a presentation with my blue-collar back ground. I didn't think people would take me seriously.

My very first presentation was the worst. I forgot my name, experienced tunnel vision and sweated bullets. Afterward, I said to Chereace that I would never be that bad again. Even though my presentation was awful, however, four people signed up.

After that day, Chereace and I would practice every night after putting the kids to bed. And I prayed about my presentation skills over and over again. Eventually I got better.

I attended my first 5LINX national convention in Niagra Falls, New York, about four months into the business. This was a huge event for me and Chereace because we'd earned promotions to the position of National Director. National Director was a big accomplishment as it was one step away from the top position in the company at that time, which was Senior Vice President.

Because we had reached National Director in such a short period of time, we went up on stage to give a testimonial before the large crowd. Again, this world was all new to me and I was scared to death. I recalled being on that stage like a deer in head lights. On one hand I was very nervous, but on the other hand I loved the stage, bright lights and the microphone. This was the start of something big!

At the convention, I met the co-founders of the company--Craig, Jeb, and Jason -- who are great businessmen. I must admit, I was a little nervous about meeting them because I didn't know if they would accept me. I worried that I wasn't "smart enough" or "qualified" to be too close to them. But these guys were cool and a lot of fun to hang out with. From day one they treated me like family and like part owner of the company. I also got to meet smart businessmen and women from all over the country and around the world.

This is when I can truly say that my mind began to expand. Growing up in the hood of D.C., I never hung out with white folks much less did business with them. Over the last four years, I've traveled the world with the co-founders and had the opportunity to meet and spend time with their wives and kids. I remember them all telling me that their vision is for 5LINX to someday become a multi-billion dollar company, and they will reach that goal by putting the representatives first.

I also met the VP of North American Sales of 5LINX, William Faucette, Jr. (former Rochester, New York, chief of staff). William is an industry expert in direct sales, and he has poured so much into my career. Today I sit in advisory council meetings with these four wise men -- as I call them -- and just think, "How in the world did I get here?"

During my years of working 80-100 hours a week, I never came first on my job. Matter of fact, I never met the general manager of my old job, and I was there for 18 years.

When we returned home from our first convention, I was ready to take D.C. by storm. I had primarily built my business in Maryland. But I envisioned bringing my message and opportunity to people in D.C. and having them respond enthusiastically.

Because of my ties to the Hyatt Regency Capitol Hill, located at New Jersey Avenue in Northwest Washington, I began renting the ballroom on Thursday evenings from 7:00 to 9:00 to present the 5LINX opportunity. After three or four weeks, few people were attending, and I began to get discouraged.

One evening I came out of the ballroom with my head down. I looked up and there was [Senator] Barack Obama with his press secretary. He had just earlier announced his candidacy to become our next president. I don't think that anyone took him seriously at that point. He didn't even have security with him. I rushed over to him to introduce myself and literally tried to recruit him for 5LINX.

He respectfully declined my offer but in his last words wished me "good luck in 5LINX." My last words to him were simply, good luck! I even used his campaign slogan, "Change is Necessary," to motivate myself and my 5LINX campaign. He becomes our 44th president, and I would ultimately go on to not only hit the Senior Vice President level, but also rise to the position of No. 1 Senior Vice President (SVP) with 5LINX. We hit SVP in July 2007. I must say this was one of the best days of my entire life.

After spending 18 years as a Metro bus driver and one year as a supervisor, I retired altogether from WMATA six months after I joined the ranks of Senior Vice President with 5LINX. It took me a mere 18 months to reach that mark and obtain financial security. Chereace retired from her federal government position about four months later.

The entire year leading up to my retirement in December 2007, I told all my co-workers and the naysayers that I planned to leave my job. I did that partially to show my co-workers that this was working for me, but mainly to convince myself that I could do it.

I remember my last day on the job. I was so scared to take that leap of faith. I had been working a job since I was 14 years old, so this was especially new territory. Even though I was making great money with 5LINX, I wondered if I could make it in the direct sales industry. What if it didn't work down the road? What if I had to go back to driving a bus?

This is when your faith kicks in. Nothing in life is guaranteed. In business, sometimes you must jump and grow wings along the way. Every businessman has done it: Bill Gates, Bob Johnson, and the co-founders of 5LINX, just to mention a few.

Chereace retired from her (GS-14) federal job in April 2008 after 22 months. Says Chereace, "I set the goal to leave my job in December 2007. I was sitting in another powerful training event and envisioning having the success that the speakers described. "Even though I planned to walk away from my job in April 2008, I really didn't know how that was going to happen. I felt extremely fearful yet very optimistic."

The following February, Chereace started her exit from the working world. She began to use the leave she had accumulated on the job. When her leave ran out, she knew she had to make a decision. "By this time it was April. I just couldn't decide what I was going to do. I felt completely torn," she recalls.

"Saturday night before I went to bed, I got down on my knees and prayed to God for an answer. God does answer prayer," she says.

On Sunday, April 6th, we all headed to worship services at First Baptist Church of Glenarden. "I will never forget that day because we were running late and I said to Stan that we shouldn't go because I didn't want to be late," says Chereace. "He emphatically said we were going anyway."

Jeffrey Johnson, a guest preacher from Indianapolis, delivered the message. He announced the name of his sermon: Which way do I turn from here? "I felt like in this moment God would give me my answer," Chereace says.

"Pastor Johnson went on to preach that in life we have three choices: 1) we can stay where we are – but we'll die; 2) we can go backwards – but we'll die, 3) go forward – our destiny is always ahead of us. Wow! I can still remember the details of that message today, partially because I've listened to the audio CD many times since that sermon. God had answered my prayer!"

Chereace knew God had something in store for her. "He wouldn't allow me to take this step without having my back," she says. "I felt confident and crystal clear that I could walk away from my good "stable" job."

On Monday, April 7th, Chereace walked into her office and waited for her boss to arrive. "When the time came, I walked into his office and said to him that effective immediately, I would be resigning from my position of Supervisory Information Technology Manager," she says.

"Needless to say, he was shocked! He asked me if I were rich. I laughed inside and boldly said no, not yet! At that moment, I felt so free. I knew God had a plan for me and no one or no thing was going to stop me. I felt unstoppable."

Her official last day of employment with the Transportation Security Administration was April 11, 2008. "That day, as I walked out of the building for the last time, I shed tears of joy," my wife says now. "I felt excited, nervous, fearful and free, all at the same time. But there was no turning back. I was a woman on a mission. It was time to celebrate! I did just that by treating myself to a matinee movie. I sat there and thoroughly enjoyed the movie as I chomped on Raisinettes and salty, buttered popcorn. This was the beginning of the best days of my life."

From the Bus to the Bentley

Chapter 14

Today Chereace and I are driven and committed to achieving the goals we've set for ourselves. We care about helping others and believe that we're examples of what's possible when you believe, decide and commit. These characteristics allow us to flourish in the 5LINX opportunity and experience incredible success.

We've hit and maintained the No. 1 position in the company for two years straight. We've helped 18 people reach Senior Vice President and one person reach the top position in the company, which is Double Platinum Senior Vice President. I believe that when you help enough people get what they want, you'll get what you want by default. I believe that teamwork makes the dream work. We wouldn't be where we are today without the grace of God and the hard work of our team.

After 44 years of living, I've finally realized who I am as a person and as a businessman. With 5LINX, I now have more time, freedom, and choices. I'm now able to do things I have never done before and would have never been afforded the opportunity to as a blue-collar worker. For me, it's not about the money or lifestyle but about what the money can do to help others.

Chereace says that 5LINX allows us to spend quality time together and with our two sons. "The 5LINX opportunity has blessed us to be a blessing to others," she adds. "With the income we've earned, we've bought a home for my parents and a home for Stan's 97-year-old uncle. We can send our children to the best schools and summer camps. One of Stan's favorite perks is taking our son to the basketball games and buying the prime "Spike Lee" seats on the floor. But more than all of that, I love the fact that I'm pouring into people and changing their lives."

Chereace's goal is to start a coaching program designed to empower women to reach beyond where they are to live the life God intended for them. Chereace recently launched her Web site and started a book club to encourage women to read materials that will expand their personal and professional lives.

Together we're establishing The Richards Group Foundation to serve at-risk youth. Another component of our foundation is going to be to create scholarships for other young people to attend the Landmark Forum. The Landmark Forum brings about positive and permanent shifts in the quality of your life. Chereace swears by the experience and concurs with other people's assessment of the program. Those who attend enjoy positive results in the quality of their relationships and a renewed sense of confidence.

We've also started Love & Business™, a coaching practice that assists couples in business based on our success strategies. Love & Business™ helps couples learn how to work harmoniously together in building a successful relationship and business. We live in such a fast-paced world. We run on the treadmill of life trying to make it all work, but in reality, most couples never spend any quality time together. I believe this is a clear reason why the divorce rate is so high. We have a formula that has worked for us, and we want

Love & Business™

Stan & Chereace conducting a Love & Business™
workshop

to empower other couples. We are creating training and coaching programs in and outside of our company and industry.

We love the flexibility and control we have over our own schedule. We set our own schedule so that we can do things that matter most. We love having time for our kids, attending their school field trips and visiting their classrooms. We can workout or enjoy a midday movie from time to time during the week while the kids are in school. We're blessed in that we can live full time and work part time.

We live by the philosophy that you can have the success God intended for you. We believe that with faith, laser-sharp focus, and action, anything is possible. We're living proof. In just under five years, we've built a network with tens of thousands of representatives all across the world and have helped many individuals obtain financial freedom and success. And we're just getting started.

As much as I love the lifestyle of being a Double Platinum Senior Vice President in an Inc. 500 company, I get my greatest gratification from helping others obtain the same success. It's good when your life changes, but it's something different when you can change someone else's life. Today I believe my purpose is to pour my experience back into ordinary people to let them know that they can do whatever they want to do in life.

Its about first figuring out what you really want. You must be very specific and detailed about what you want. I found out that most people never get what they want out of life simply because they don't really know what they want from life.

Once you take the time to find out what you really want, you must begin to get uncomfortable with yourself.

In order to get comfortable in life, you must first be willing to get uncomfortable. Chereace always says that if you do what's easy, your life will be hard, and if you do what's hard, your life will be easy. We've learned that success and living life on purpose isn't easy but it's worth the effort. Not only can you live the life God intended, but you also can position yourself to make a real difference in another person's life. We feel tremendously blessed and excited about where God is going to take us.

From the Bus to the Bentley

Chapter 15

If I had to sum up in one word what the journey to this point in my life has been about, I would say transforming. I've gone through highs and lows and have learned a lot along the way. The following six life lessons have helped me overcome obstacles to reach this place of transformation:

1. Faith. We all must have faith in God to succeed in whatever we want to do in life. To me, faith is all about believing even if you can't see the end result yet. It's hard to believe in something when you can't see it, but that's what faith is all about. Next, you have to act on that belief. According to James 2:20, faith without works is dead. Faith is critically important, but you have to act on that faith, not just sit back and wait on something to happen. Reflecting back over my life, I exercised faith when I tried out for one of the twelve spots on the AAU basketball team. More than 140 kids from all over the city tried out for those spots. I knew that if I worked hard, I could make the team. And I did. Another time I exercised faith was when I attended day and night school to graduate on time. I maintained this rigorous schedule all while working full time at McDonald's. This was a challenging time for me but I had the faith that if I worked hard, I could do it. And I did. After my salvation, when I was at the lowest point in my life, I really leaned on my faith as I surrendered to the Lord. I believed that even though I had hit rock bottom, my faith in Jesus would carry me through this storm. And it did! When I started 5LINX, I had faith that I would succeed even though I couldn't see it in the beginning. I couldn't see true success because I had never spoken in front of people. I'm also not technical and barely knew how to turn on a computer. I had never met anyone who had made it to the top of a company like this, especially someone with my background. I exercised faith and leaned on the belief that God would give me what I needed to succeed in 5LINX. And He did!

2. Discipline. I've learned that an ounce of discipline outweighs a ton of regret. I've learned that the hard way. As I was growing up, no one modeled discipline in my household. I did what I wanted to do even as a child. I went to school when I felt like it and stayed out as long in to the evening as I desired. There were no rules....at least in my mind. When I entered the workplace, I struggled due to my lack of discipline. I just couldn't get to work on time. I now believe my tardiness was due to my lack of discipline. I've had many regrets in my life. But I've learned how to master self discipline in order to achieve what I have thus far. I've learned how to make short-term sacrifices in order to have the long-term gains.

3. Humility. I've learned to get rid of my foolish pride and embrace humility. God loves humility. Most people never get ahead in life because of foolish pride. I embraced humility on several occasions in my life. First was when I was fired from the Metropolitan Police

Department. This was the most humiliating experience in my life. To be escorted out of the building in front of my team was devastating. Getting a security officer's job in a hotel afterward and facing the same co-workers, now commissioned officers, was tough. I wanted to hide under a rock.

A spirit of humility allowed me to persevere in the face of adversity and ridicule. True leaders humble themselves and take the necessary actions to move beyond their situations. In the MPD academy, I was on top of the world. I had my Corvette and expected to join the ranks as a police officer. My life changed in an instant. After this downfall, I even went back to the FBI to ask for my former job back, even though I didn't leave the bureau with a good track record. Now, that's humility.

4. Position. We must position ourselves around successful people who have what we want. Building relationships is key to reaching the next level in life. I was always good at making friends and aligning myself with key individuals. I realized early that you are the sum total of the five people that you hang around most. Most of my friends made 100K yearly, after working hours of overtime. I like to call them hundred thousandaires! Nothing was wrong with this, but I realized that if I was going to the next level in business and in life, I would need to begin hanging around people who were where I wanted to be and had the lifestyle I wanted.

When I started 5LINX, I was able to do that. My relationships with the co-founders and other leaders in the company allowed me to dream bigger and expand my vision and level of thinking. These relationships helped me step outside of my comfort zone.

165

I've learned that success is usually waiting for us when we step beyond what's comfortable.

I've learned so much in the last five years just by positioning myself with the right people. It has helped me expand my vision of what's possible. We must stop hanging out with folks who don't share our vision. Once you position yourself around the right people, ask the right questions: How do I get to where you are? How did you do it?

5. Vision. Vision is all about seeing or imagining the future as you want it to be. Most people can't see past their noses. If you don't have vision, you'll end up anywhere. In other words, don't live life by chance.

My vision growing up was to just get out of the "hood." I just wanted a good job with a steady paycheck, my own place, and a nice ride. I just didn't know what I could really have out of life. And when you don't know, you don't know.

My vision expanded once I positioned myself with the leadership in 5LINX. My vision grew as I grew in the business. Initially, my vision was to make $2,000 monthly in 5LINX. Then it expanded to leaving my job, which occurred 18 months after I got started in 5LINX. Now that I've obtained financial independence with this company, my vision is to help 100 people become millionaires.

Vision allowed me to see myself as unstoppable and capable of doing whatever I put my mind to. There's a saying: "Once the mind expands, it will never be the same." My expanded vision allowed me to see a world that I never knew existed. A world full of possibility.

All the major business players we know of today have vision. Bill Gates (Microsoft), Bob Johnson (BET), Steve Jobs (Apple), the owners of 5LINX -- Craig, Jeb, and Jason -- all had big visions for their companies. When I started 5LINX I had no intention of leaving my job. I bought into Tishina's dream because she envisioned quitting her job.

Then I met Lisa, C. Anthony and Barry Donalson, and my vision grew from making $2,000 a month to not only quitting my job but also becoming financially independent. If you have a small vision, then position yourself around people who have big vision.

6. Character. Character is about possessing qualities such as integrity. It's about doing what you say you're going to do when you said you were going to do it. In business, character is important because people do business with people that they like and trust. What I found is that people must buy into you first before they do business with you. If you don't have good character you won't go far in life. I believe you get out of life exactly what you put into it. In other words, you reap what you sow.

My lack of character caught up with me when the police department fired me. This was a turning point for me in this area because I realized I couldn't go any further than my character. Most people don't reach their true potential because of a lack of character. When my character was righteous, I excelled. I obtained stable employment with Metro, and later my businesses really took off. All because of my renewed character.

I hope this book inspires others to follow their dream —or

at least not quit! They can use me as an example and say, he didn't quit, so why should I? Two of the greatest gifts I received from God were drive and determination. Three of my top accomplishments were graduating from high school, beating my drug addiction and reaching Senior Vice President with 5LINX.

"He'll move heaven and earth to help someone. He'll give you the shirt off of his back. He's a very classy guy and at the same time business savvy. I'm so proud of him," summarizes Reese, who, along with her husband, is now one of my National Directors in 5LINX.

I want all the youth in the inner cities to read this book because I believe it will give them hope. I want people with any type of addiction—substance abuse, alcohol, gambling, sex—to read this book and get their lives in order. In order to truly get your life in order, you have to know and embrace the power of God and Jesus Christ. You must clearly understand that if nothing changes, then nothing changes. You must be open to change.

I want the blue-collar workers—sanitation workers, taxi drivers and barbers [just to name a few]—to read this book. I want those brothers [and perhaps a few sisters] to know that your job is not the end all! Don't define yourself or let others define you by your job, position or title. You can still go out, use your creativity and develop your own wealth.

Think outside the box! Write that love story or book that you have been meaning to do. Record that song you've been singing to yourself all these years. Complete that invention you had in mind several months or years ago. Embrace your fears and stop running away from them. Right beyond your fear is where you'll find your success. Fear comes from Satan, not God.

I encourage college students not to define themselves by their degrees. Even though I didn't go to college, my wife did, and she realized that she limited herself according to her degrees. Chereace learned she could do more than build information technology systems. On one hand, she discovered a lot about herself in college and wouldn't change a thing about her experiences. On the other hand, she found that even though she excelled in her academics, she allowed her major to cloud her vision and potential.

Corporate white-collar employees must understand that in 2011, you can no longer rely on your title or degrees. These days, you must go out and create your own wealth. That six-figure income that you started with 10 years ago won't work today. Chereace learned that the hard way when she experienced a layoff unexpectedly in 2002.

All of us must step out of our comfort zones and decide to win. Remember that a failure is someone who quits before the journey ends. The only way to lose is to quit.

I was reminiscing recently about my life. If I could go back in time and change some things, I would never use drugs. I would also be more disciplined during the earlier part of my life. I would take my education much more seriously and I wouldn't waste so much time looking for shortcuts in life and avoiding responsibility. I would also go back and apologize to anybody that I hurt and tell them it was unintentional.

I would like to be remembered as a man of giving and serving—a man who loved the Lord, a faithful husband and a devoted, involved father. I want people to recall a man who was a great leader who led by example. I've met plenty of men with money who aren't good husbands, fathers or entrepreneurs.

I always knew as a child that someday I'd be financially free and in a position to do some great things in life. And here I am. Thinking back now, I must credit my shero Doris Olivia Richards, because she used to instill in my subconscious mind as a young boy that "You're great! You're a conqueror! You're a leader! And you're a great man of God!" Even though back then I thought she was kind of weird, her words resonated in my subconscious. With that in mind, watch what you say to your young kids.

If someone could use this book to inspire and show youth, particularly African-Americans in impoverished areas, how to invest in themselves and not rely on others for success, I'd be ecstatic.

I want to inspire our youth to learn how to meet new people. Sometimes they seem to get stuck in a rut. If a new person isn't a homeboy or homegirl from the same neighborhood or part of town, kids appear reluctant to befriend them. Meeting new people with diverse backgrounds and interests, however, helps you grow and expand.

Think about it: I met Tishina Pettiford, who introduced me to Lisa Cloud, who introduced me to industry experts Barry Donalson and C. Anthony Harris, then the co-founders of 5LINX, Craig, Jeb and Jason. Through this new circle of friends, I've written my first book five years later. All of that was the result of a willingness to meet someone new.

Young people must learn and master the skills of asking the right questions when they meet or network with people. Once they accomplish these skills, they must distinguish and determine what kind of people will best help them achieve their goals and ensure success, and build that relationship. Too many times young people leave important life-changing decisions up to chance without having a solid plan.

Our youth also must learn that charity begins at home. I host an annual event called Fam Jam. It's a family jamboree or special event where all the males over 30 play a competitive game of basketball with the males under 30 years old. After the game, I give out trophies before we partake in a cookout featuring some of the finest barbecue and fixings.

The purpose of this annual event is to allow the entire family to fellowship and focus on the youth, particularly the males. Random discussions come up about creating new possibilities and goals for the males in the family. In addition, I invite a male guest speaker to the event to share their story and inspire the attendees.

My future goals during the next five years are to help develop 100 millionaires in the direct sales industry. For more information about this effort, e-mail me at stan@fromthebuestothebentley.com. I know this will happen through faith, focus and action.

I also want to go back to the inner city of Washington, D.C., and teach entrepreneurship through the Richards Group Foundation. My plan is to first make people aware that they can do whatever they want to do. I will have them search deep within themselves and reveal what they want to do or become. I will then commit to work with them to create a realistic game plan to achieve their desired goals. I'm a firm believer that our kids just need caring people to show them they can do whatever they want to do in life!

As my brother Cornell would say, "Yesterday is history.

Tomorrow is a mystery. Today is a gift. That is why we call it the present." Make sure you use your presents wisely.

Part IV

From the Bus to the Bentley

Discussion Questions

From the Bus to the Bentley

Chapter 1

"My father would come over in the middle of the night stalking my mom. He even kicked down the front door of our apartment a few times."

In this chapter, the author recalls spending the majority of his childhood battling poverty and hunger as he and his family relocated from place to place around the city. He changed schools frequently and had no stability in his life.

Discussion Questions

• How did your past shape who you are today?

• What did you learn as a child about family, marriage/relationships, or finances? Did you learn positive or negative lessons?

• What do you recall most from your early classroom years? In what ways do you draw on what you learned back then?

Bonus Questions

- Do you allow your past upbringing to dictate what you can have today or in the future?

- Have you been dwelling on the past rather than learning from it?

- Have you ever made a poor decision based on negative lessons you learned in the past?

Chapter 2

"I was shooting craps when I looked up and saw momma staring me in the eyes. She grabbed me by my aftro and dragged me down the steet."

The author changed schools many times during his elementary school years, which didn't instill a love of learning. Because of his neighborhood surroundings, he developed a habit of compulsive gambling. However, he also discovered his talent for basketball, which gave him direction and joy. His coaches taught him life lessons that he has passed on to his children.

Discussion Questions:

- Think about some of the positive and negative habits you might have developed as a child. How have these habits affected your life? Has a negative behavior or habit ever cost you something important? What are you doing to address any remaining negative habits?

- What sorts of talents or hobbies did you develop as a child? What did you enjoy doing as a youngster? How are you using those gifts today? Knowing what you liked to do as a child can help you identify your real purpose in life.

- Do you believe you received a good education as a child? Why or why not? Have you succeeded in life because of or in spite of the education you received?

Bonus Questions

- Do you know your true passion? What brings you joy? What are your best skills -- those attributes for which you often receive compliments? Taking time to identify your true talents, gifts and skills can help you take advantage of new opportunities.

- How have your past experiences developed your character? How can you use those experiences to launch out in a new direction or help someone else? Think of ways to reframe a negative occurrence and turn it into something that benefits you and others.

Chapter 3

"I learned an important life lesson from my senior-year experience. Ask for what you want openly and with conviction, and if God deems it right for you, you'll get it."

Basketball helped the author escape the pain in his life, but only his younger brothers ever saw him play at an organized game. Despite the lack of family support and the disappointments he suffered, he kept going. Friends, mentors and faith made the journey a little easier.

Discussion Questions

•   Who are the members of your support system? How do they help you overcome discouragement or disappointment? How do you support others?

•   Describe the qualities of a true friend. Do you have such people in your life? Are you a true friend to someone else?

•   Which educators/mentors encouraged you along the way and helped you get where you are in life?

From the Bus to the Bentley

Bonus Questions

- The author suffered a major disappointment at age 14 when he tried to get money to travel to Las Vegas with his basketball team. Think of a major disappointment you have suffered in life. How did you overcome it? Does the memory still weigh on you today? Have you forgiven those who hurt you? Most important, can you leave that hurt in the past and move on?

- The author recalled how hard he worked to graduate high school. How have you overcome a major challenge in your own life? If you're still facing a major battle, who do you have on your team to help you? Write down the resources you have at hand (friends, family support, and so on). Most important, how can your faith help you get past your obstacles? Think of ways to strengthen your faith and encourage yourself.

182

Chapter 4

"I was still a teenager and not legally able to buy beer in a night-club or from a liquor store, but my future seemed bright and I was all smiles. perhaps everything came too fast for me, and I couldn't go anywhere but down."

After completing high school, the author had to decide what to do with his life. Forgoing the path to college, he entered the work-force by getting a job at the FBI. His new job and higher salary led to a new car and his own apartment. But the opportunity also revealed character weaknesses that would soon prove to be a problem.

Discussion Questions

- As a child, what lessons did you learn from family members about spending, saving, investing or donating money to charity. Can you recall anyone specifically teaching you principles about money or business? Did the adults in your life say one thing and do another? How have those experiences affected your relationship with money today?

- As you entered the workforce as a young adult, did you believe only certain career paths were open to you? Or did you think that you could become anything you chose? Where did you get these ideas and beliefs?

- What is your definition of success?

From the Bus to the Bentley

Bonus Questions

- Stan Richards felt discontent at his job before he began working at the FBI. Do you feel stuck or unhappy with where you are right now? How can you get moving again? Brainstorm some possible solutions. (For example, you can envision where you want to be; set specific goals; sign up for a course; or talk to a coach, counselor or pastor)

- The author said he went on a spending binge after he got his first job and found himself sinking into materialism and debt. Have you ever spent beyond your means to project a certain lifestyle or treat yourself because "you deserve it"? What was the result?

Chapter 5

"Cocaine lied to me and made me believe that I got confidence from it. It was pure evil."

Stan Richards' good streak came to an end as he experienced problems at work and engaged in the party lifestyle. Despite the warnings and pleas from older relatives, he used and eventually became addicted to cocaine. He was ashamed of his habit but didn't know how to escape it.

Discussion Questions

• Because he grew up without a father, the author had no sense of discipline in the workplace. How have experiences from your childhood -- both positive and negative -- affected you on your job?

• Is it ever appropriate to play the "race card"? Whom should we blame for issues and problems in our community: society, ourselves, or something else?

• What can you do to develop a greater sense of discipline and willpower in your life?

Bonus Questions

- Looking back at your own life, can you identify those times when you might have sabotaged your own success due to fear or a sense of inferiority?

- Stan Richards' uncle warned him to stay away from cocaine, but he didn't listen. In your own life, do you regret not taking someone's advice? What was the result? How did you overcome any setbacks?

Chapter 6

"When I woke up that Monday morning, my only concern was how to get that cocaine out of my system."

Ignorance and pride kept Stan Richards from seeking professional help for his addiction while at the FBI. He kicked his habit long enough to join the D.C. police academy, but his old lifestyle soon caught up with him.

Discussion Questions

- How has a lack of fathers and male role models affected our communities? Can you see the effects of this problem in your own life?

- How did the author's peers play a role in his downfall?

- The author said he slipped back into his old tendency of wanting to be the center of attention. Can you identify character flaws and tendencies that hold you back? What strategies do you use to overcome them?

From the Bus to the Bentley

Bonus Questions

- Stan Richards asked God why he had participated in behavior that could jeopardize five months of hard work. Why do you think he put himself in such a precarious position?

- How can a friend, coach or accountability partner offer vital assistance when you feel tempted to go off track and blow all of your achievements in a moment? What other strategies do you use to manage your emotions and maintain self-control?

Chapter 7

"I had no job, I was behind on my rent, and my childhood sweet-heart left me for good. All my dreams appeared to be dying one by one."

Stan Richards hit the ground running to find a new job, but he soon experienced another setback. At this point, his life seemed like one big question mark.

Discussion Questions

• Stan Richards says he and his brothers inherited an incredible work ethic from their father. Can you name some gifts, talents or characteristics you've inherited from your family that have helped you succeed in your career or business?

• Why do you believe the author sought yet another job in law enforcement?

• When his D.C. law enforcement career ended, the author felt a range of emotions: anger, disappointment, anxiety and finally depression. Reflect on what you experienced when you faced a major setback in your own life.

Bonus Question

As all his dreams appeared to die one by one, Stan Richards felt depressed. List some positive tools you can use to encourage yourself if and when you face your next challenging situation.

Chapter 8

"At the end of the revival service, I went to the altar. the anointing of God was so intense and fervent, you could have cut it with a knife."

A dead-end job, horrible credit and a less-than-perfect living situation: Stan Richards existed in a funk of depression as he dealt with the consequences of his choices. But all that changed when he experienced deliverance and healing during a revival. Going cold turkey from cocaine, he got baptized and focused on building a new life.

Discussion Questions

- Do you recall the family and friends who helped you find your way back from a devastating situation? How did you express your gratitude? How are you helping others recover from job layoffs, health crises or other challenges?

- How did the prayers of the author's mother prevail in this situation? How does his testimony show the value of consistent, fervent prayer?

- If you've lived long enough to experience some problems and setbacks, how do you look at life differently now? What did you learn about gratitude, humility or responsibility? Would you now describe that challenge as the best thing that ever happened to you?

Bonus Question

- "A failure is someone who fails with no hope, and a winner cannot be a winner without accomplishing something that involves effort." Doris Richards often shared this advice with her son, Stan. What does this statement mean to you? Have we mistakenly learned that success is easy? Perhaps we admire the successes of others without considering the process they endured to achieve their goals. How can you encourage yourself to keep pursuing your dream despite obstacles and barriers?

Chapter 9

"I continued to pay off all my debts and renew my credit. Now that I was focused on the prize and not on the dope, everything I did had purpose."

Stan Richards walked the straight and narrow path as he sought to get his life back in order. Co-workers, friends, and even a local sportscaster motivated him and helped him stay on track. And getting hired as a Metro bus driver was like a resurrection from the dead.

• The author worked as much overtime as he could to save money for his own apartment and eventually his own home. What is your No. 1 goal right now? List the steps you're taking to reach your objective. What are you doing to stay focused and avoid distractions?

• The author also kept a simple schedule/routine to stay focused and avoid negative influences and acquaintances. How does your lifestyle help or hinder the goal you have in mind. Putting your daily or weekly routine on paper might help you identify problem areas or extra time in your schedule you can use to reach your goal.

• Stan Richards said he prepared for the opportunity to work at Metro. Describe in detail how you are preparing yourself for your goal.

From the Bus to the Bentley

Bonus Question

"You don't always have to cross the finish line first to prove that you're a champion. Just cross it and you become an automatic winner."

- What does this statement from the author mean to you? Many of us think success has to arrive or appear a certain way. Are you open to alternative paths to your goal? Are there routes and ideas you haven't considered? If you reach your goal at age 60 instead of age 30, are you still a success?

194

Chapter 10

"I had showed the haters that I had made it back from the depths of depression and hell. Life should have been perfect -- but it wasn't."

As Stan Richards got his life in order, he began to experience rapid changes both professionally and personally. Some ventures worked -- and some didn't. He experienced both rewards and challenges as he attempted to learn about business and life.

Discussion Questions

• Although Stan Richards didn't like working as a security guard at a hotel, the insights he gained from that experience inspired him to create a new business venture. How can you do the same? Brainstorm ways you can use previous experiences to create a new income stream for yourself.

• A lack of closure on his traumatic past derailed the author's marriage and ultimately led to divorce. How have your previous experiences affected your relationships? Why is it important to make peace with the past before starting something new?

• Have you ever talked yourself out of a good opportunity? Looking back at that experience, what could have helped you make a better decision? What strategies have you put in place to assist you in making good choices? (For example, mentors, an accountability group, fasting and prayer, and so on.)

Bonus Question
• Through his encounter with Les Brown, Stan Richards learned that he was afraid of success at that time. Does the idea of actually reaching your goal overwhelm or frighten you? Why? Listing your fears and concerns on a sheet of paper can give you some clarity and perspective.

Example: If I become successful, my extended family members will think I've changed and become jealous. Or, if I become successful, people might have expectations or demands that I can't meet. Or even: I'm afraid to succeed because I'm afraid of somehow losing everything and looking like a fool.

Journal your thoughts. Do these fears make any sense? You can get additional help from a friend, coach, mentor or counselor.

Chapter 11

"Even as a child, Chereace always desired more out of life. "I had dreams for my life, and working a 9-to-5 for 30 to 40 years wasn't part of the vision," she says.

When he least expected it, Stan Richards met his wife and soul mate, Chereace. Like Stan, she'd experienced some setbacks and disappointments. Giving her life to Christ and spending some time developing a relationship with herself gave Chereace a new out-look and prepared her for her husband.

Discussion Questions

- Although she enjoyed college and always wanted to try new things, Chereace said she suppressed her sense of ambition until much later in life. Are you holding back certain aspects of your personality due to fear or unbelief? Are you trying to live up to others' expectations? How can you get free of those constraints?

- Has a lack of direction or purpose ever led you to make a poor decision? What was the outcome? How can we learn to develop a sense of purpose for our lives? If you haven't done so, spend some time developing a mission/vision statement for your life.

- How did spending time by herself prepare Chereace for a new

197

relationship?

Bonus Question

Even as a child, Chereace always desired something more out of life. "I had dreams and visions for my life, and working a 9-to-5 for 30 to 40 years wasn't part of the vision."

Can you list some of the dreams and visions you have for your life? Or have you stopped dreaming? List 10 things you'd like to accomplish before you die. Let your imagination run wild!

Chapter 12

"We had the niceties that come along when there are two incomes in a household. We had the "stuff", but no time. "

A lunch date on a beautiful sunny day led to a wonderful courtship and eventually marriage for Stan and Chereace Richards. However, although they had good jobs, great kids and lots of stuff, they had no time. A family crisis forced Stan Richards to ask: Had he found real success?

Discussion Questions

- As a "blue-collar worker," Stan Richards experienced a lot of emotions watching Chereace navigate the corporate world. How does our image of ourselves impact or hinder our personal and professional success?

- Stan and Chereace seemed to have it all, but they had no time. Can you identify some things in life that are more important than money/materialism? (For example: freedom, flexibility, health or time with your children.) How are you making those things a priority in your life?

- A layoff prompted Chereace to pursue her goal of becoming a business owner. What spurs you to pursue your goal? How do you keep that reason at the forefront of your mind? What tools can you use for encouragement when you encounter obstacles? (For example, you can write motivational messages on sticky notes and post them all over your home. Or you can cut inspiring pictures out of magazines and create a visual reminder of what you're trying to accomplish.)

Bonus Question

- After her layoff, Chereace found a job that provided security and a good income. But she still didn't feel fulfilled. Write down what a fulfilling life would look like for you. Would you launch a business? Go off on the mission field? Pursue another educational degree?

Chapter 13

"If you want to go to the next level in life, you have to position yourself around people who have what you want."

Discussion Questions

- The Richards had a negative outlook on direct sales prior to getting into 5LINX. How does their story inspire you to keep an open mind?

- To succeed in any business, you need a humble, teachable attitude? Can you set your pride aside to learn from someone else? Reflect on a recent example.

- "If you want to go to the next level in life, you have to position yourself around people who have what you want." What do you think of the author's statement? Assess the family and friends in your inner circle. Do they meet this standard? Do they inspire you to fly or keep you tied down with fear and negativity?

- Stan Richards had to overcome his fear of public speaking to make business presentations. What fears must you get past to succeed in your career or business? Learn from Stan and keep practicing and praying. Don't give up!

Bonus Question

Both Stan and Chereace had to find the courage to leave their former jobs and work their business full time. All business owners must learn to take thoughtful, calculated risks. Have you done all your homework? What resources will you need? Who can help you launch out into the deep?

Preparation is important, but at some point you will have to take a step of faith. *"Nothing in life is guaranteed. In business, sometimes you must jump and grow wings along the way."* -- Stan Richards

Chapter 14

Today Stan and Chereace Richards strive to achieve their goals and help others. Through their business success, coaching practice for couples, and foundation for at-risk youth, they've established themselves as examples of what's possible when you believe, decide and commit.

Discussion Questions

- "For me, it's not about the money or lifestyle but about what money can do to help others." Think about the author's words. What does true wealth mean to you?

- Can a couple maintain a successful business and a marriage? What are the pitfalls? If you're married discuss with your spouse some ways you can stay focused and committed as you build a future together.

- According to Stan Richards, most people never get what they want out of life simply because they don't really know what they want from life. If money and time were no object and you could do what you wanted, what would you do and have? (For example: travel, charity, homes, cars, college for children, help others, pay off bills, vacation, give to your church, and so on) Use this time to identify what you really want in life.

203

- A goal is a dream with a deadline. Decide what time period you would like to achieve the preceding goals. Choose one year, three-year, five-year, and 10-year goals.

Bonus Question

The author says, "In order to get comfortable in life, you must first be willing to get uncomfortable." Success and living life on purpose aren't easy, but the results are worth the effort. Are you up to the challenge? Discuss with a mentor, coach or trusted friend some ways you can get uncomfortable in order to eventually obtain the comfortable lifestyle you desire. Ask that person to hold you accountable.

Chapter 15

Discussion Questions

- What does faith mean to you?

- How do we conduct business differently these days? What specific changes have you noticed in your particular industry? How have you adapted to these changes? Have you been open to trying something new or are you resistant?

- "A failure is someone who quits before the journey ends." Spend some time thinking about your views on failure. How does the idea of failure make you feel? Is it part of success -- or the worst thing that can happen to anyone? Examine the lives of such great "failures" as Thomas Edison or Abraham Lincoln. What do they teach you about perseverance?

- What are you most proud of in your life right now?

Bonus Question

- What will you do in the next 30, 60 or 90 days to make your dreams a reality?